He Walks His Talk

In researching *The Living Dreamer*, we have conducted interviews with hundreds of successful managers of large and small companies and have been impressed with certain and specific outstanding examples of emerging entrepreneurial enterprises that embody and employ the principles that he has outlined in this book. Here are a few companies that Mr. Angelson has helped us in assisting to deploy. Mr. Angelson works as the executive liaison and assistant to the partners of these affiliates.

Global Digital Information, Ltd. is on the cutting edge of development and marketing of computer software for Internet and document imaging applications.

Ukrainian-American Development Corporation—The principals of the company have been involved in opening markets in the Ukraine for over five years. They have emerged as the largest steel exporter in Ukraine and are now beginning the make acquisitions in the privatization process going on in various countries. Imagine being able to go back in time and position yourself for profit in the infancy of today's giants like IBM, McDonalds, Coca-Cola, Microsoft, GM and others.

Cavendish Bentinck Limited—Investment bankers and transfer agent. The foundation of this European company is based on the thousand-year-old name of the Cavendish family, who are well known throughout the British Commonwealth for their history of fortitude and integrity.

Atlantique International Investment Bankers—Specializes in startup for early stage development high technology finance, particularly in Eastern Europe and China. This company focuses on hands-on incubation of business opportunities in computer, Internet and medical technologies.

Medical Research and Marketing—Finds and funds cutting edge medical technologies on three continents, bringing late-breaking medical diagnostic and treatment equipment to market while lowering costs to patients.

The Living Dreamer

The Art of Doing It

Copyright © 1997 by B. Angelson

The Living Dreamer™ and
Human Engineering® are registered trademarks.

First Edition
Printed in the United States of America

This book is part of the works of B. Angelson. It is presented to the reader as a record of observations and research into the human mind and its languages, and not as a statement of claims made by the author. This book is based on the author's practical personal experience and does not purport to provide psychological counseling.

All rights under International & Pan-American Copyright Conventions, no part of this work covered by the copyright herein may be reproduced or used in any form or by any means—graphic, electronic or mechanical, including photocopying, recording, taping or information storage and retrieval system—without the written permission of copyright holder or the publisher except for use in the usual reviews.
All rights, domestic and foreign, reserved.

Publisher's Cataloging in Publication
(Prepared by Quality Books Inc.)

Angelson, B.
 The living dreamer : the art of doing it / B. Angelson.
 p. cm.
 Preassigned LCCN: 96-78124
 ISBN 0-9651590-3-5

 1. Self-actualization (Psychology) 2. Self-realization I. Title

BF637.S4A64 1996   158.4
                                    QBI96-40393

Book design & graphics; cover graphics: Carol Lindahl
Excerpts from the literary works of Diana Lee—
"A Dream, The Beginning," "The Coming of The Dreamer" and "Become Your Dream"
Cover design: Latent Images
Cover model: Autumn Star
Photography: Beaux Art Studios

Do It Publications, International

Seattle • Los Angeles • New York • Milan • Hong Kong • Tokyo • Paris • Sydney • Frankfurt

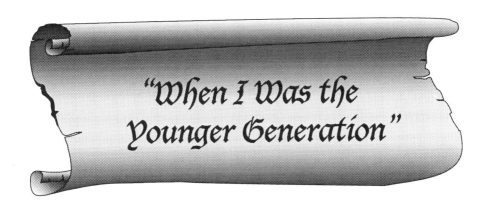

"When I Was the Younger Generation"

"When I was the younger generation
I set out to change the world.
When I grew a little older
I perceived that this was too ambitious
so I set out to change my state.
This, too, I realized as I grew older
was too ambitious, so I set out to change my town.
When I realized I could not even do this,
I tried to change my family.
Now as an old man I know
that I should have started by changing myself.
Had I started with myself,
maybe then I would have succeeded
in changing my family, the town,
or even the state—and who knows,
maybe even the world?!"

— A Great Wise Man's Last Saying

Contents

Preface xiii
A Dream, The Beginning xix
Step I –
Purpose 1
Adventure I –
The Horizon Concept 13
Promise Yourself
Step II –
Goals 17
Step III –
Silhouette of Success 31
Adventure II –
The Principles of The Living Dreamer 45
Step IV –
Desire—How Badly Do You Want Something? 53
Step V –
Self-Image—Do You Like the Image In the Mirror? .. 65
The Coming of The Dreamer 81

Contents

Step VI – Self-Discipline 83

Step VII – Relationships With People 89

Adventure III – Merlin and King Arthur 103

Step VIII – Possibility Thinking 105

Step IX – Creative Imagination 117

Step X – Stickability 127

Step XI – Explosive Enthusiasm 137

Step XII – Producing Results 145

Flying in a Dream 159

Become Your Dream 161

All poems with no author noted are from *The Treasures of The Living Dreamer.*

Dedication

To my lost, departed brother, Kenny, who always told me that, "It's not how many times you get knocked down, but it's how many times you get up that counts."

To my father, who allowed me the opportunity to type on his typewriter at age four; who has tried to get me to put my correct finger forward always.

and

To my loving mother, who has told me and still does, "That I could do anything I set my mind to—Yes! Even fly like King Arthur as the hawk."

Preface

Dear Dreamers,

ongratulations are in order! From the moment you made the decision to read this book, you stepped out of the crowd of mediocrity. And this indicates your desire to be a winner! You have just taken the first step into an incredible and successful journey towards becoming a new person.

Every person is born to dream and to utilize what they have been born with. Though all are created equal, each individual has the opportunity to become greater by unlimiting their own future. Everyone's future is important, because that is where they are spending the rest of their lives.

Becoming a winner and being successful begins within—in the mind—and comes to fruition through our actions, which generate our accomplishments. The fundamental truths of Nature that are inborn within each of us, will be explained so that you may live your life to its fullest capacity. Your willingness and determination to apply the principles within these pages will improve your life. You will be given the knowledge, understanding, and motivation to fulfill the dreams that until now have only lived in your imagination.

You will realize that you are sitting at the controls of a vast power source—*your own mind*. We have a mind that would shame a computer! Scientific research has proven the human mind storage capacity is approximately ten billion units of information compared to the most advanced computer. Explore the dormant mind and expose more of your talents by learning about how the mind works. You will be directed in cultivating your best capabilities, which will lead you to a successful, happy, meaningful future.

The Living Dreamer

If you are finding this hard to believe, then perhaps your inability to picture success for yourself is because you have been conditioned to believe that it was not meant for you. Do you feel you are not capable of achieving great things? Because you cannot picture yourself up front, do you take a back seat? Has mediocrity washed you away? Then it is time to put aside the handicaps and barriers to what you can be. When an individual is willing to recondition their mind, plan a purpose for their life, and want it with a burning desire, they can reach new pinnacles of success. Heights can be reached that now exist only in the depths of dreams or on the hazy horizon of tomorrow.

People are born with dynamic abilities. All of the necessary ingredients for success are within each of us. We can achieve success when we believe and dare them to happen. Where we land, in the history books or on the unexplored planet of our dreams, is completely up to us! Why wait for our dreams to materialize? They will not evolve by themselves. We make them happen. When we do not, we'll probably still be waiting for our lives to change many years from now.

How does one begin?

Begin with a purpose. Once a purpose is determined (what one would like to accomplish and become in life), one can then move forward with an organized plan to achieve it. All of the tools you will need are now within your reach. However, your commitment is absolutely necessary for these principles to work.

If you do not think you have a purpose in life, then your entire existence is about to change. Do you have an unsatisfied urge or some forgotten desires, maybe some ideas still undeveloped?

Now is the time to bring your neglected aspirations back into focus, regardless of how old or outmoded you might think they are. You now have the means to realize your dreams.

The literal purpose of *The Living Dreamer* is to assist all who come its way to discover their purpose in relation to their abilities and interests. It has been planned to progressively lead even the most negative, despondent, discouraged individual to become an

The Living Dreamer

assertive, goal-oriented and independent individual. A definite purpose can and will expand and improve anyone's life.

We believe that the prime mover of Humankind is a purpose that involves helping others. Time and again it is found that in the climb to success, no man, woman or child stands taller than when they bend down to help another along the way. It is not the duration of one's life, but the donation one makes to life that counts.

The "world" within...

The Living Dreamer's philosophy is based on proper attitude towards living, love of self and others, organized action, teamwork and unity of purpose. All are shown to be essential in motivating people out of dull routines and nonproductiveness and into meaningful and rewarding lives.

While the world appears to be in fast-forward with jet transportation and modern communication, the "inside world" of Humankind is, for the most part, undeveloped. We can transport ourselves at lightning speed, but we have yet to conquer and communicate with the vast riches that live within our own minds.

You will be given the map and the specific guidelines on how to improve your life. It will require your desire and determination to achieve what is possible for you.

As you become involved in your own plan of self-development, you will desire to participate in goals that are not just for your personal benefit, but are also those of assisting others. You will be discovering specific objectives for yourself and those dearest to you. Some of our greatest contributors in life are those who are setting a worthwhile example for their family, friends and community, and who enjoy the image of respect and guidance. This is our philosophy—the belief of people helping people to greatness!

All of the individuals within these pages are real people. They are your "guides" and inspiration to show how lives can be changed and how these concepts of Nature will work when given the opportunity. Once you apply these principles to your life, they will work for you,

xv

too. Why would anyone wish to remain on an unchartered course in life when proven ways are now known to exist?

The success of this adventure depends on your success. When you become successful, you contribute to the success of others and your country. There is a need to be filled, right now. There are needs to be awakened in each of us. Many of us sell ourselves short and never realize our limitless potential. How can a country utilize its full capacity when the leaders of tomorrow are accepting mediocrity rather than being dynamically motivated to purposeful action? You can be part of a great awakening by believing something can happen to you and through you. Be good to yourself, for there is only one you.

Let the knowledge within this book educate the undeveloped person within you, being your "President in Charge of Personal Achievement," assisting you in achieving your best in life. Yes, you were born to dream! Believe it.

B. Angelson

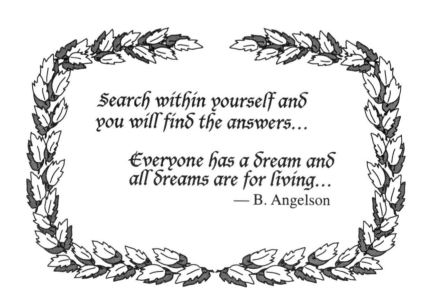

Search within yourself and you will find the answers...

Everyone has a dream and all dreams are for living...
— B. Angelson

A Dream, The Beginning

I looked at the reflected image in the mirror staring back at me, making direct contact with my eyes. Only this time, I was looking at myself objectively—through the eyes of another.

"My, how you have grown," I complimented out loud. Everything about the person in the mirror seemed quite different. As beautiful as...a dream?

Almost in the same instant, I remembered just how much my appearance had changed from when I was young. That ugly duckling story is not just something that I had heard as a child. The truth is, my entire existence is like that of a fairy tale. It was not so long ago . . .

Every day seemed exactly the same. I got up, went to school, then went straight home. Actually, it was more like a house than a home. I was lonely. If there was anyone around, I often felt even more alone. No one seemed to notice me. I felt like I was different from everyone else. Not special—I was a very plain-looking child—I just thought I was different.

The only place I truly lived was within. If it were not for my active imagination, life in its entirety would have felt pointless. Growing up seemed the hardest part of surviving in this seemingly detached, uncaring world. So I learned to share with myself. I lived the life that I dreamed of in my mind, and believed in it so much, it has come full circle.

If it were not for the isolation from the outside world when I was young, I would not have entered and developed the world that exists within. I would not have come to know and understand who I really am, and what I am capable of. I have come to the realization that no matter what kind of circumstances that exist in life, good or bad, they exist for a definite reason.

We are all here on our own path in life — here to grow, and learn, and share what we know. Our lives will cross paths with other lives. When these paths intersect, knowledge and understanding will be exchanged, and everyone will benefit. I have learned that all of us have the same capabilities I have discovered on my innermost journey. However, it will be completely up to you to utilize the knowledge that is now being given to you. No one can live your life for you.

The world within, the intangible universe of mind, of thought—unconscious or not—is a place where one has to experience to be able to understand. A person cannot comprehend the vast complexities without observing it on their own and within themselves. Words cannot convey, but they can be the tools that one needs to "travel" and explore the incredible domain that exists within each and every one of us. Just as every individual has his or her own personal physical identity, each also has creative uniqueness within. And once the inside (mind) of a person knows the way to travel—the outside (body) will then be able to transcend and become all that is possible.

Who am I? Why am I here? These are questions that come to everyone sooner or later. Whether we are looking in the mirror or "looking in our souls," we long for the answers, and these will be different for everyone. The person you are meant to be exists right now in the dreamy world of your imagination. Bring "that person" into the daylight of reality.

Who you are and what you become is solely up to you. Once you discover who you are, then your life will become all that it is meant to be. All of us have a definite purpose in life. I have found mine.

As best as I can, I will unfold the knowledge that has brought the beautiful changes to my life. The little "ugly duckling" that was my image in the younger years has become an exquisite creation, as the miraculous wonder that I have come to understand within my own mind.

Love does conquer all that it touches. And it begins with love of self. It changes, and somehow rearranges what seems ordinary, into a beautiful kind of living artwork. There is, after all, a "Dreamer" within everyone.

Let us begin.

Step 1
Purpose

One of the first things that any person needs to start improving his or her life is a purpose. It is when one has a definite purpose that there is some direction in life, that the right decisions can be made and the right opportunities can be pursued.

Two of the greatest and most rewarding satisfactions in life are 1) becoming who we wish to become and 2) accomplishing what we desire. Can you honestly say that this is where you are in your life today? Are you even on your way, with a purpose in sight? Do you think you are truly the kind of person you are capable of being? Are you in touch with the dreams that live in the inner resources of your mind? And are you doing anything to make your dreams come true?

Take some time right now and run through these questions in your mind. You must decide on what you believe, what you desire out of life, and what you can contribute to this life. This is your beginning. This is your foundation. A definite purpose will be the starting point of your accomplishments.

It is time to get a heading on your course and mark your point of destination. Do you have a purpose in life? If you do not, then you will learn how to acquire one in the steps laid out in this book. Do you have any unsatisfied urges, forgotten desires, or some undeveloped ideas? Any living, breathing individual should have some aspirations, or at least a desire or two! If you cannot think of any, recall a time in the past when you enjoyed thinking of them, even if the passing of time has washed them away.

Sometimes it is hard to know what one's true purpose is. If you cannot think of one immediately, do not despair. For some of us, it takes a little more time and effort, for we have not as yet discovered

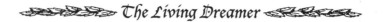
The Living Dreamer

who we are and what we are capable of. When the time is right, it will come to you. Just keep your mind open to all of the possibilities. Who is to say what is or is not meant to be? Remember though, that if it is something that is dear to you, something that you desire very much, then try for it. You never know. If you can't imagine others believing it, that is no reason for you not to try to live your dreams. This is your life, and the dreams you have are yours for a reason.

The Wright Brothers had an unusual idea. They believed in it so strongly that they developed it from a thought to a purpose in life to be attained, even in the face of ridicule and repeated failures. They believed a person could dominate the sky and would fly.

It has been said that another person had the same idea for a machine that could fly through the air. The truth of the story is that he had his plane, in his barn, ready to fly one year prior to the flight of the Wright Brothers' plane. He had never flown his plane because no one else had ever done such a thing before and he did not have enough belief in this dream to be the first one to try. Because he did not believe, he did not try. He did not dare to make his dream happen and become the first to venture and face the risk of failing. He flew his plane the day after he heard about the successful Wright Brothers' flight—too late to land in the history books! The greatest ideas without belief and action never soar into orbit.

It is time to bring your neglected aspirations back into focus regardless of how you think others might react to them. Remember, we are all individuals on this earth, and all of us have our own unique abilities and interests. If we do not express ourselves and do not try to fulfill our dreams, then our lives will not be lived to the extent that they have been gifted for. Others will not be able to admire and learn from our accomplishments. Make your dreams your purpose. Set your sights high enough to reach your target, aim, and squeeze the trigger!

Life can be everything that we could ever imagine, or it can end up being nothing but a dull existence. We are the ones that have the "keys" to unlock and unleash all that is within us. We will never know what life could mean and how much there is waiting just for us, until

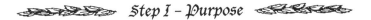
Step 1 - Purpose

we decide to start living up to our potential. When we know our potential, we will have a better understanding of what our purpose is.

How does one know what his or her potential is? By asking some questions, and being honest with the answers. The answers will give some direction.

Ask yourself questions like:
- What do I enjoy doing?
- What are my fears?
- How do I really feel about myself?
- What are my talents and skills?
- What am I best at?
- When am I the happiest?
- Where do I need to improve?
- What do I really want out of my life?
- Is there something that I want to accomplish?
- What dreams do I have that would change my life if I pursued their existence?

It is very important to keep a daily journal, *and everything must be written down!* The answers may even change as we continue to grow and improve. This journal is an excellent way to not only focus on what we want, but seeing it in our own handwriting makes us acknowledge that we really want it. This also gives us the opportunity to really think about ourselves. We then have a record of how we are doing, every day, and of just how much effort we have been giving. It is a confidence-builder, a means to express ourselves and learn all we can about who we are.

This journal can be our guide as to what is important to us, what we are interested in, what our abilities are, and give us direction. It will also give us the encouragement and incentive to keep going. You may even discover that you have more going for you than you ever imagined.

Learning about ourselves is like an adventure, and it is made up of one step at a time. There is no need to be afraid of what will be found, for all of us have barriers to climb and handicaps to overcome. It is the learning experience that we need to enjoy—not just whether or not we succeed every time.

The Living Dreamer

Once you establish your worthwhile purpose, ask yourself if you possess the self-confidence it takes to accomplish it. A majority of the people do not. Don't follow this majority. Why follow them when you know they do not exercise self-confidence? Especially when self-confidence is one of the most vital vehicles in accomplishing one's purpose.

Without self-confidence the greater part of our abilities are asleep. Are you ready to wake up your abilities? Confidence is an acquired quality. These pages are laid out for you to establish this confidence in yourself.

Now, do you have a backbone or a wishbone? What is the backbone after all? It is that set of bones where one's head rests on one end and one sits on the other. It's completely up to you which end you use the most.

Picture your life as a rubber band. You can allow it to dangle in its natural state, or stretch it out just short of breaking. The outer limits of your achievements and your contributions to living must be your purpose. You have amazing abilities waiting to be released, exercised, and experienced.

Instead of having either envy or admiration for those who are using all that is in their domain, start using all of the gifts still "unopened" in your possession. You have had these gifts since the day you were born. They are like precious stones, gold and pure silver. Take out all of the "treasures" you have been fortunate enough to receive. Use them, that is why they have been given to you.

So define your purpose and completely commit yourself to achieving this purpose. A definite purpose is an absolute necessity in order to make a contribution to life and an impact on life.

Try searching out great human needs and make this a better world by filling those needs. Let the answers come from within, from your feelings and your heart. Goodness and kindness will flow when you suppress non-productive actions and become a part of a cause greater than yourself.

There is no greater satisfaction in life than knowing people need you, and that through your unselfish efforts you are serving someone's needs. There is also a deep gratification derived from knowing that each time you serve another person, you serve your inner self even more. One of the most beautiful and surprising joys in life is that there

Step 1 - Purpose

is no way you can sincerely help another without helping yourself. The people who can forget themselves in serving others become much better people in the process. Forget what you have done for others, but never forget what others have done for you. You can always receive happiness when your attitude and desire are to serve.

The sages of old have said that when people pray for others, their own prayers will be heard first.

While you are working to help, assist, encourage and motivate others, observe what it will do for you: "A righteous man," said the wise, "his work is done by others."

You can participate in great achievements as others have, others who have dared their dreams! You can change a dull existence and make your life meaningful! So many people have slipped into a rut. Do you know what a rut is? It's a grave with both ends kicked out of it! Certainly you have no desire to fall into a rut?!

Your purpose is your reason for living, for waking up each day and being thankful to be alive, and *thankful to be you*. Why be like most of the people you meet? When you listen too much to the average person's ideas, you might find yourself in the same predicament as the individual driving over a bridge. When he saw someone about to leap, he cried out, "Don't jump! Come down! Let's talk it over!" They talked it over and then they both jumped!

In these steps, successful men and women will share their best with you. Like you, they have dreamed. Then they turned their dreams into reality. You can also launch the most seemingly impossible dreams, chart them through the sea of development and see them arrive in the port of realization. Your dreams will become your tangible reality.

People of all ages and from all walks of life are hunting for life's treasures. But so many are like the child who finds an old treasure map in the attic, goes out and makes all the "left turns and right turns—by the limb when the moon is high and the light beams hit the ground, dig down three feet and find a treasure." After locating the treasure chest and removing it from its hiding place, they carry the chest inside and say, "Look! I've got a treasure!"

You can't ignore the fact that once you own the chest all of the treasure inside is yours. But what so many people fail to realize is

5

The Living Dreamer

that ownership of the chest is of no value until the chest is opened, the treasure brought out from inside and then something is done with it! It does not matter how great the value of the treasure is, for it is worth nothing until it is put into productive and constructive use.

You already have this treasure within. You are the sole owner, and no one else possesses anything exactly like what you have as a unique individual. In this book, you will be supplied with all the tools you will need to open the "lid," so you can start using what is inside of you without any further delay.

Begin right now to think about a purpose for your life. If you have a definite long-range purpose, great! This will be a blueprint for your future. Draw the lines carefully, for each mark must have meaning. If you do not have a purpose, decide on one for the immediate future, then add one stone at a time. Soon you will have erected a dynamic, structured purpose for your life.

Ask yourself the question, "Do I have a purpose for my life?" and if you cannot think of one, then use this one to get started:

My purpose in life is to completely and totally understand myself and all other healthy beings within my present and future environment, while maintaining and creating my body in perfect health, now."
Sign:_____Date:_____

This is to say that you have set your sail and a course in life that will outlast the physical life span that has been given to you by Nature. Sign and date this one, for it is guaranteed to reach out that far, and more, for you.

Everyone should decide who they really desire to be, what they desire to accomplish and what they desire to contribute. A worthwhile purpose will guide you by providing you with the incentive to travel each mile of your journey. It will change you by giving you zest and enthusiasm in your day to day living as you progress ever forward. And a worthwhile purpose will set you above the crowds that have settled on the plane of complacency. You will know where you are going and will learn how to get there.

6

Step 1 - Purpose

Why be like those who don't know where they have been, much less where they are going? With direction, your life will have more meaning, be more comprehensive, and have greater depth.

You stand on the threshold of achievement when you start with the desire to go forward. Analyze and determine where you stand in life. You will find there are a couple of main directions, or avenues, you can take:

1. Surrender your will and desires and accept the will of other average people, the will of the masses trapped in a dull routine. No discoveries will be made, no conflicts solved, just "follow the leader"—the leader who is smart enough to be different. You will live your life building up this one leader while you stay behind to play the role of the "average" individual.

-OR-

2. Be "Creative" with a middle initial "S" for success! Be the one who succeeds in accepting the realization of having a purpose and following it to a fulfilled complete success, no matter what "Average" has to say!

Statistics reveal some shocking facts. A group of one hundred people at age twenty-five all anticipate success. The same people can be found at age sixty-five: one rich, four independently wealthy, five still working, thirty-six dead and fifty-four flat broke. Of those reaching sixty-five years of age, eighty-five percent have less than six hundred dollars. How is it that in the richest nation on the face of the earth, only five percent are considered successful?

A great philosopher is quoted to have said that the reason individuals do not succeed is that they simply do not think.

There is one principle philosophers throughout the ages have agreed upon. It is this: "As a Man thinketh in his heart, so is he."

Simply stated—*we become what we think.* Look around you. Do most of your acquaintances prefer conformity to creativity? Where has it all started? It is no doubt in the way they condition themselves to think.

Appoint yourself as "Chairman of the Board" of your faculty, which is composed of your body and actions. As the boss, first recall all of your nonproductive thoughts, and body languages (habits, mannerisms, etc.) that still occupy "seats" in your establishment. Second, redirect your own thinking and guide "the board" to follow your original ideas and proposals. You have the authority, and all eyes are on you for your first design!

James Russell Lowell said, "It is not failure, but low aim that is a crime in life."

The Roman Emperor and Stoic philosopher, Marcus Aurelius, more than eighteen hundred years ago, said, "Our life is what our thoughts make it."

You need to decide on a definite purpose. It can be both materialistic and idealistic in thought. It is like the pot of gold at the end of the rainbow of life, the oasis in the middle of the desert. You strive diligently forward, knowing you must always keep the vision of it before you.

Purpose is like a "golden thread running through the tapestry of your life." It is of a lifelong endurance and provides form and substance in the bustling panorama of daily activities. It is the ingredient that turns "a castle in your dreams" into your dreamy castle in reality.

In this step, several references have been made to the untold number of people who drift down the sluggish stream of mediocrity. Instead of a sparkling, bubbling current of daily living, they slog through streams polluted with unhappiness, discontent and dullness.

What is the "formula" that can transform your life from minus to plus?

1. You can step over the dividing line between mediocrity and success right now. Cross over on a "bridge" called *purpose*. By exerting only a small amount of extra effort and time with a purpose in mind, you will pull yourself out of the mediocre group. Those who have "made their mark" in this world, whether financial or in any other area, have not always done so because of an unusual ability or talent. So many times it is as simple as exerting just a little bit more effort than others are willing to put forth.

   This brings us to another very necessary point when considering purpose. Since our total purpose invariably involves work (often our occupation and means of earning our livelihood) it is very important to enjoy what we are doing.

Step 1 - Purpose

2. When our purpose brings us to activities we don't enjoy, then it is wise to re-examine that purpose. This is intertwined very closely with number one. How can you exert that extra effort needed to create that successful achievement when you loathe what you are doing?

   Someone anonymous stated: "I honestly think that everyone should make it a point to do work they enjoy. They should find out what their aptitudes are and follow them, wherever they lead." With this encouragement in mind, proceed to the next step.

3. Plan each step, one at a time, like a "stairway" to your purpose. True, you may only be able to see the first two definite steps, but as long as you keep the pinnacle of your purpose in sight, you will always be headed in the right direction.

   Reaching our purpose is much like starting out on an automobile trip at night. We know the end of our journey, but can see only as far as the end of our headlight beam. Only when we have gone that far, can we then see a bit further. So it is—one portion at a time is illuminated, until we reach our destination. "Plan your work, then work your plan," is applicable here.

   How many times have you heard the saying: "Don't bite off more than you can chew"? A delicious and bountiful repast can be enjoyed, when it is taken one mouthful at a time.

   When you try to take forward steps that are too big, you raise your risk of failure. Then, when you fail, you fall back and become discouraged.

   Some people have an unconscious desire to fail. They do not plan and do not stretch their abilities to fulfill their plans. They make feeble efforts, or even none at all. And when they don't succeed their alibi is, "I didn't really try."

   Others remain in a rut. They never put themselves to a test by making definite plans and then sticking to those plans. They don't know what they can do, because they have never made an honest attempt to do it!

4. Know that there will be times when problems will be so great you will fail to accomplish some definite plan. Learn from these failures. Leave them behind you and go on to ultimate success. Just

The Living Dreamer

because there is a "detour" on the road doesn't mean you have to quit your journey. It only means there is another route to travel.

When we never fail, we will probably never learn. To never fail often indicates we are operating within our capabilities. When you can go beyond them, you stretch your abilities just as much as you can. You actually take a giant step forward, breaking the conformity mold.

Almost everyone learns as much from problems and failures as he or she does from success. Only the person who has failed to gain insight from failures has truly a lack of know-how. Just think of failures as a detour toward success. It's okay to fail sometimes, as long as we have made an effort to succeed. We will learn things about ourselves that, if we never made an attempt, we would never know.

One underachiever who has become a millionaire stated, "I failed in business three times before I became successful. It's not how many times you fall down that counts. What counts is how fast you get up!"

5. Follow the examples of others who have succeeded. Recognize your weaknesses and buttress them with the help of people who excel in the areas in which you fall short.

The successful results of many great Americans are examples of this: Shipbuilding has been revolutionized in our time by an individual who had only five years in a classroom, Henry J. Kaiser. He hired others to work out the technical details for which he did not have the training. Eddie V. Rickenbacker, famed race driver, World War I flying ace, and later the president of Eastern Airlines, knew the areas he was less strong in and looked to others to become part of his endeavors.

You need not be born an executive to follow this principle. When you are in the working field and have difficulty, or when you must do a lot of public speaking and feel you are not getting your points across to your audience, or in any situation where you are weak—look to those who are strong. Search out and analyze the secret of their success. They also had a departure point. You are standing today where every great person stood yesterday.

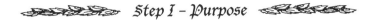

Step I – Purpose

Tomorrow others will be admiring your achievements. Ability is fine, but the ability to recognize ability is even better. When you take what you know, add to it what others know, then you are twice as smart as you were before! Never be afraid to ask someone, whose wisdom you admire, when you need guidance.

6. Consider any opportunity in relation to your total purpose. When the opportunity opening before you is a one-way street and it will not help you progress toward your ultimate purpose, then you are better off not taking it. Perhaps one of the most difficult steps to take is to move away from a "blind-alley job." Any time you are in a rut, quit whatever it is that is keeping you there. However, it is important to weigh all factors, especially how they fit into your total plans for achieving your purpose. In other words, don't jeopardize your livelihood before you are ready.

   It is well to keep in mind that financial remuneration is not always the total reward. Often the experiences you gain from one job will make your later income much greater.

7. The final ingredients in this formula for improving your life are these:
   a. No rule for success will work when you don't.
   b. To get along with others, go along with others.
   c. To progress toward your purpose, think for yourself.
   d. Don't procrastinate. Make a plan, and stick to it as much as possible. Procrastination makes an easy task seem more difficult.
   e. Plant and cultivate good constructive/productive habits or body languages. They will work hard for you at no extra cost.
   f. Resting on your past successes will not produce a better tomorrow for you.
   g. When you desire to leave footprints in the sands of time, wear work shoes.

The Living Dreamer

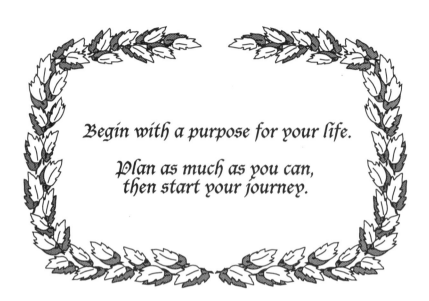

Begin with a purpose for your life.

Plan as much as you can,
then start your journey.

Adventure 1
The Horizon Concept

There once lived a great king, a long, long time ago. This masterful king was known for being very wise. This king had a son of whom he was quite proud. He spoiled him like fathers do, giving him almost his every whim.

On one of the king's frequent trips to the seashore, the king took his son with him. As usual, like any child, his son became interested in the many things that the land around the sea presented to him. He was like most children, in that respect, a very inquisitive youngster.

The king's son had his own private teacher responsible for explaining all of the things of the world to him. One day the king's son summoned his teacher to his side.

"Oh, great teacher, what is that 'line' out there where the ocean and sky touch together?" said the young prince.

"That line, Sire," said the wise old mentor, "is something called the horizon."

"I don't understand," said the young prince.

So the wise teacher explained over and over again, but to no avail. All of his attempts to explain the meaning to the child were in vain.

The king's son finally said, "Bring it to me so that I may touch it."

"But that's impossible, Sire," said the mentor.

The young prince, always accustomed to having his own way, went crying to his father. "Father! Father! I want that line out there and no one will go and get it for me!"

The king, besides being very wise, was also very patient. He also did his best to explain it to his son, that to bring him the horizon was physically impossible.

13

The Living Dreamer

However, that did not satisfy the youngster either. The boy refused to give up. He wanted that "line" and could not understand why his father refused to give it to him. He always got what he wanted. He cried and cried until his father finally decided to satisfy his son's curiosity in the only possible way he knew.

The king ordered one of his ship's captains to take his son aboard ship and travel west. He was to travel in that direction until he was sure that his son was satisfied that he understood the meaning of the horizon. That is, to understand that he could never physically capture it, or touch it, in any physical way.

The captain, having to obey his king's every wish, did his master's bidding. He sailed westward toward the setting sun with the young prince aboard his ship. The captain thought as the king did, it would not take the young prince but a short time to see the folly of his wish.

However, the young boy would not give up. Westward they sailed. Days, weeks, and months passed. Naturally, they had to set goals to stop for food, water, and other provisions, as they continued on their voyage into the westward sun—attempting always the impossible feat of physically touching the horizon.

The trip took the young prince to many strange and interesting places. The boy grew much wiser than others his age, as they traveled into the unknown. Eventually, they circled the globe and returned to the home port.

The young prince understood now that he could never physically touch the horizon no matter how many times he circled the world. He learned from the experience that it could only be touched in one place. That is, in his mind on its picture chamber's screen (the imagination).

The king's son told his father of all the adventures that he, and the crew of the ship, had shared on their journey. He told his father of all the unknown worlds that existed far from the sight of the king and his subjects. He told of the different lands they had visited on their journey.

The king, being the wise man that he was, knew that he could not completely understand the experiences of his son. For he himself had not been there in person, but he was glad that his son went away a child and returned a more advanced thinking individual.

Adventure I - The Horizon Concept

Our purpose in life must function like that of a horizon—forever visible, but untouchable in terms of our physical or tactile senses. Our life purpose functions in the invisible world of our mind, but the end result shows up as a body language, in the visibly physical, sensual world of our existence. Purpose, like electricity, is invisible to our eyes and we cannot physically touch it. We see only the end result of both. Electricity presents light and we see it. Purpose presents a body language and it is visible, also. Each "glows" and manifests as something. One is of glass and metal, and the other is of flesh and bone.

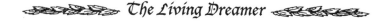

The Living Dreamer

"Promise Yourself"

"To be strong that nothing can disturb your peace of mind.

To speak of health, happiness and prosperity to every person you meet.

To make all your friends feel that there is something special in them.

To look at the sunny side of everything and make your optimism come true.

To think only of the best, to work only for the best and expect only the best.

To be just as enthusiastic about the success of others as you are about your own.

To forget the mistakes of the past and press on to the greater achievements of the future.

To wear a cheerful countenance at all times and give every living creature you meet a smile.

To give so much time to the improvement of yourself that you have no time to criticize others.

To be too large for worry, too noble for anger, too strong for fear, and too happy to permit the presence of trouble.

Who is too wise? The one who can learn something from someone else."

Step II
Goals

Alan O. was making headway in his ambition to be a disc jockey, and was doing an outstanding job passing on his voice to others in voice-over commercials. Alan was a human dynamo with only a few outlets. But he was quite shy and hesitant about engaging in any activity that required personal initiative or self-confidence.

Alan had often heard the "super achievers" tell of their accomplishments in the business world, but he saw them as personality individuals, gifted far beyond ordinary people. Then one day he became aware of The Living Dream— a philosophy that appeared somewhat ordinary and not yet polished in its presentation of success. But he had heard that it was a great teacher for all of the qualities he desired for himself, and he realized it would enable him to become the person he really wanted to be.

As Alan learned of its philosophies and principles, he thought, "When others can do it, in of all walks of life, then I can do it, too!"

There was one thing lacking—the goals that are imperative to direct him towards the greater arenas of life's achievements. His goals were not defined, and he was not yet aware of his latent talents.

Once he became involved, he began making the necessary decisions for goals of personal initiative and accomplishment. He took on a completely different personality. He lost his shyness and became an aggressive "go-getter." He evolved into a great individual who could manage his business and was willing to take the risk of profit and loss—in other words, to risk his neck to become an achiever.

The Living Dreamer

How many "Alan O's" are out there somewhere to be discovered? The world is overflowing with them! Now it is your turn to be turned on to all you can be. Your own greatness is only a few steps ahead.

Every successful person became that way by setting goals and working hard. No one ever attained anything by accident. To accomplish something you have to set a course and stay with it all the way.

One of the outstanding rewards of having goals is personal happiness. Life is too short to be unhappy, and there is no way one can be happy until a worthy, challenging goal is achieved.

A famous writer stated: "Our generation won't go to the moon. The next generation will talk about it, but they will not go up. The reason is that we don't believe we can."

John Fitzgerald Kennedy made the statement: "This nation should commit itself to achieving the goal, before this decade is out, of landing a man on the moon."

You must also believe you can successfully achieve your purpose. You must prove it by setting goals. Just as President Kennedy believed we could reach the moon, so did the workers in NASA. A goal was set. We reached it in 1969, because we believed we could and we set out to do it! Set your goals and let nothing slow you down.

Again consider the question, "Are goals necessary?" Look to the world of sports. What is it that makes football, basketball, hockey, or any other game a contest? Is it a certain number of players moving back and forth across a set area? No, it most certainly is not!

The goals are what make the game. Remove the goals and everything becomes a meaningless shuffle, regardless of how much action is generated.

The goal is always quite visible and clearly defined. The players know which way, and how far to direct their efforts. Any game would have little interest to you without having a definite purpose and the goals which attract the action and provide the challenge.

The purpose of the game is to win through sportsmanlike effort. To achieve this purpose is to continually move forward and meet the challenge of the goals. Athletes who have no interest or dedication to score by reaching the goals no longer function as athletes. Spectators have no interest in watching them and they are soon left to their unorganized (goal-less) activities.

Such is the game of life. Only those with commanding, worthwhile goals enjoy participation in the action, grow, and continue to a satisfactory finish.

Concentration or Specific Single-Point Focus Goals

You have just read how goals are necessary for the success of a group. The individuals participate as parts composing the whole of the group. The focus of a goal will be different for the success of a single individual.

So the question may be asked, "Are goals necessary to me?" It has already been pointed out that goals provide direction, just as signposts along a road keep the traveler on the correct course. From the position where you are now, and looking at the ultimate end—your purpose—goals provide the "shortest distance between two points." They enable you to progress toward your purpose in a more or less straight line. They help to prevent wasted time and energy by restraining you from wandering down dead-end trails that may look profitable, but actually are not productive and decrease the speed of your advancement.

There is great power in the ability to mentally concentrate with single-point focusing on a single idea, until you decide to discharge the thought from your mind. Concentrate, with all of your mental energy, on one goal at a time.

Goals have often been defined as, "the place where incentive is to be found."

What basic quality do individuals have who are a pleasure to be around and who vibrantly enjoy life? What is it that dull, uninteresting, listless people do not have? The one quality that is the bedrock of productive life is incentive.

Incentive is that which encourages or urges one on to a particular action. Goals provide incentive to move, to act. When these goals are reached, through personal endeavor, they become a source of fulfillment and also spur you on to the next goal.

19

Goals make the difference between a lackluster, tedious life, and a sparkling, daily adventure. Goals are the force that energize behavior and give a person focused direction.

Are goals necessary? This can well be answered by quoting an anonymous humorist who said, "Those who aim at nothing hit nothing!"

Remember: No great or worthwhile purpose has ever been achieved without goals.

What Are Goals?

It has been said that people are always desiring something and doing something about their desires. Since the chief trait of human beings is desire, then their desires are their goals! This, however, is only a partial explanation of goals. There are times when we are quite unaware of what our desires and goals really are.

"What am I trying to do?" is a question too searching for many to ask, much less answer honestly. One thing we must bear in mind—all behavior is an attempt to reach some goal, whether or not we are fully conscious of that goal.

Often it is only in books that an individual's goals are simple, clear and orderly. Perhaps in your own life they are confused and often in conflict.

Then where might one begin to construct a framework of goals? A good place to begin is with goals or desires that can be put into words, when you are aware of what you care about, and what interests you. This awareness comes through an overall purpose (discussed in Step I).

Most of us know, or at least have an idea, of what we desire. We know it will require our effort to overcome the obstacles along the way, and can anticipate what satisfaction the end-state will bring. When there are risks involved in achieving our purpose, goals help us calculate and control those risks. Goal-behavior is clearly purposeful.

Goals must be personally decided. Even though two people appear to have the same goals, it may be discovered on examination that wide differences exist. Even similar goals for different people will be

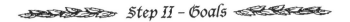

Step II – Goals

manifested in different ways since they each see their situation from their own unique vantage points.

A goal-directed activity is controlled by your conscious and deliberate intention to achieve certain objectives. You achieve these by means of a specifically chosen course of action.

What is a goal? A goal is first of all deciding what it is you desire. What is it that is most important to you? Secondly, it is facing the question, "Is what I desire worthwhile?" Your answer concerning these questions will determine whether you are ambitious or greedy.

Ambitious people desire things for themselves and their loved ones, but they are willing to pay a fair and honest price for that ambition.

Greedy people desire something for nothing and don't mind who they trample on to get it. Decide today in which direction you are headed because your attitude in this decision will place you on either the right path, or the wrong path.

Wordtracks

Wordtracks, or thoughts, are the organized information. Think of them like the tracks that a train runs on. The train can only go where the tracks take it, and the tracks are laid with a destination in mind. And just as people lay the tracks for where the train is to travel, their thoughts (unconscious or not) will decide on where they will go.

Goaltracks

Goaltracks are the plans which are laid by writing them down. This will determine the direction of where the wordtracks (thoughts) are to go.

Timers

A goal without a stated completion date is like faith without works—dead. Procrastination at work. The goal can never materialize because of its infinity timer. The same type of time that's in the "I will drop it" phrase:

Hold a pencil between your first finger and thumb and say, "I will drop it," and repeat it over and over for about fifteen seconds. Notice that while you are saying the phrase "I will drop it" over and over, the pencil remains between your finger and thumb. Even though you presumably told yourself that you were to drop the pencil, it remained where it was. Now, say to yourself, "I will drop it on the count of five." Now count to five, but notice that between one and four it remains between your thumb and finger. Then, on number five, it releases. In the "I will drop it" phrase there is no time of when it was to drop from between your finger and thumb—except infinity. When you stated a specific time for this to occur, that is the only time when it could happen.

Keep in mind that long-term goals can hardly arise in connection with the incentive to obtain purely personal pleasure. Your goals and object of life must be with an awareness of intent to contribute that which is positive and good, or you will find yourself on the receiving end of that proverb, "Whatsoever a person soweth, shall that person also reap."

Are Goals Necessary?

You may have previously been taught that the way of the majority is the correct way. In this step it has been stated that the majority are drifting, missing out on much happiness and a rewarding life because they do not have a goal-directed life. Since establishing goals is an activity of the successful minority, then would it be considered a "normal" action to formulate and maintain goals?

When examined on a very elementary level, setting goals is merely organizing our time and actions. We all recognize the organized activity of the enormous expanse of the Universe, often dramatically illustrated in our space-oriented society.

Men and women are like the Universe itself. We are also of a purposeful dream of people's smaller hopes and dreams (our parents). All existence is innately or naturally goal-directed toward goal objects.

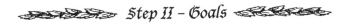

Step II – Goals

The animal setting out on a foray to fill its goal, such as that of satisfying hunger, accepts such as an integral part of its life.

Both animate and inanimate objects have goals. Trees either shed their leaves or grow new ones, depending on which "goal-behavior activity" they are in. Birds fly north or south in the proper season, accepting these instinctive goals naturally. These are just a few examples to illustrate the natural, basic need and acceptance of goals, which are innumerable.

People also have goals, and the striving to meet these goals is rooted in their inherited nature. Some goals are related to their physical needs. There is a goal in their desire for food and shelter, for protection and security. Even their nervous system gives them the means of making adjustments and reaching specific goals. So you can see that goals are very much a part of our natural constitution.

Although our physical being (fundamentally and independently of conscious control) is goal-oriented, there are other normal goals not in our physical state. The need for goals is also shown in our personality.

"The existence of goals in human life is the third great characteristic of personality." (Anonymous)

A personality strives for specific goals. Goals provide the substance that combines all elements to produce a unified, unique and recognizable personality. We would build a personality only as strong as a brick building put together without mortar, were it not for this essential ingredient called goals. Just as cement is necessary to make a strong, lasting structure, so goals provide the "glue" to keep the structure of our "building" sturdy.

When events reveal a series of means and ends, the idea or concept of a goal develops. The explanation for any action with an end in view, is that you are striving for a goal. This is one reason why a clear understanding of our goals helps us to direct our actions.

Our psychological system is such that our natural functions are greatly improved when we have definite goals. However, sometimes these goals have to be brought to our attention by someone or something else. How many times have we heard it said, "I work better under pressure"? Is it pressure that causes this increase in productivity? No, it is an external force that has set the goal for the person. Once faced with the challenge of meeting that goal, the individual will then apply themselves diligently to the task.

One of the purposes of this step is to help you develop into a mature person, meeting your major, long-range goals with the satisfaction of an endeavor well done, as you move through a series of short-range goals.

A mature individual is someone who:
- Realizes that he or she is naturally a goal-oriented person;
- Accepts establishing goals as a vital part of life;
- Formulates the necessary goals from within, without waiting for any demanding external conditions.

Setting Individual Goals

Goals are divided into two major categories: long-range goals and short-range goals. Another name for them could be remote goals and immediate goals, respectively.

There will be times when a purpose will cause goals to be in conjunction with each other. A good example of the combination of the two is the student who enters college in order to begin medical training to become a doctor. The student knows what the profession of medicine is and what courses must be passed in order to be properly trained.

Here we see immediate goals forming a chain for a long-range goal. Latin may be an obstacle to overcome, but the student assumes the risk. One must have an awareness of the goals and that awareness provides the incentive needed to accomplish the purpose.

At this point, it is well to heed the fact that just because you can define and talk about your goal, it does not necessarily mean it is the only goal being sought. Even with a clearly defined outward or social goal, many times the inner goals are still complex and not so clear. When this is your situation, remember—this is not uncommon and it has a way of solving itself.

Immediate or short-range goals may be trivial. For example, to have the car serviced tomorrow. Remote or long-range goals are often

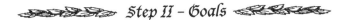

Step II - Goals

more vital to the life purpose. They tend to organize themselves into a larger system, or a "plan for living." Goals seem to have a way of "hanging together" with some consistency. This is why, when you have one clearly defined goal, the goals that are more obscure will begin to take shape.

The important thing is to decide what you desire to do, and then do it! Your interests and values will determine much of what you do, exerting some control over your more immediate goals.

It is very important to project your individual goals in ways that demand action:

1. Write out in one sentence your lifelong purpose and what you desire to achieve (do this right now if you have not done it yet).
2. Have a year-by-year progress checkup with your family, friends and business associates.
3. Plan a week-by-week program of action. This will include relationships with others and your own physical fitness.
4. Plan your week on the Friday before the actual week. You can double your production by scheduling effectively.
5. Focus on improving your day-by-day personal achievement.
6. Live in "day-tight compartments." Don't let yesterday's failures affect you today, and don't let tomorrow's anticipated situations worry you out of today's achievements.

Establishing and Maintaining Goals

Goals become the means to check our progress. They also act as "magnetic" points, drawing us ever closer to our destination. We can achieve long-range goals by working through short-range goals, which will add inspiration and fulfillment to our lives.

These smaller-in-scope goals check and balance the progress of our long-range goals. They should be scheduled weekly, monthly and semi-annually. When you fail to meet one of your short-range goals, if it is for a solid and justifiable reason, don't be overly concerned. Remain focused on the long-range goals and this will help you overcome any short-range frustration.

The Living Dreamer

Whether long- or short-range, your goals should be:
- Written, shared, and committed
- Realistic and attainable
- Concrete and measurable
- Flexible and reflect change
- Extended to cover certain time periods
- Set in advance

Fill out goal cards (3" x 5" size is excellent) and display them. Your goal cards should be on the bathroom mirror, the car sunvisor, or in your wallet. Engrave them deep into your mind (your active file) by always having one where you can see it. You must stay with your ideas until they become a part of you. Then every action will (consciously and unconsciously) be directed toward achieving your goals.

Our goal-thoughts can be used to crystallize our thinking. We are now in the position to crystallize and clarify our thinking, in order to gain a better perspective. This helps for us to realize what is important to keep, and what must be discarded, when we are to accomplish our worthwhile goals.

Remember, the word is crystallize—*not fossilize!* There are too many fossilized relics of the disasters of the past. These goals are your "lifeline" to bring you out of a boring, sluggish existence, to the thrilling experience of knowing you have succeeded in your endeavors.

You must constantly remind yourself that goals provide the steps for accomplishing your specified purpose. Every interim climb along the way is another notch on the ladder as you climb toward your success.

Follow this procedure:
1. Set one goal, or several, to be achieved in one year.
2. Decide what is needed to accomplish the goal(s).
3. Set monthly goals that lead to your yearly goal.
4. Keep a record of achievements (including a timetable).
5. Learn from any failure in the past, but do not let it slow you down.
6. Avoid wasting time. Once it has passed, it can never be reclaimed.
7. Stick with your goal until it becomes a reality.

Step II - Goals

Develop a clear and concise plan to accomplish your goals. You can begin with collecting the facts and information that will support the goals. Study every detail until you can write out the major accomplishments that are required. Next, determine how you will accomplish your goals. Set an approximate date for each completion. Review your goals periodically. Continue to check on your progress toward their completion. Keep this information recorded in your daily journal. This is a wonderful tool for introspection, reviewing, and for reviving. Self-confidence will be growing with every page that is written and every time you read your past entries, acknowledging how far you have come.

Be sure your goals challenge every part of you, and then maintain the drive that will accomplish each goal on schedule. Such attainment comes from total commitment. Your total commitment turns every goal into a stepping stone to keep you steady along the way. It also lets us realize the importance of keeping immediate goals flexible. Since the circumstances of life have a way of changing from day to day, so must goals be structured to withstand certain changes.

Our behavior will be displayed in ways which seem most likely to bring us to the goals we have set. When outside circumstances change our behavior, even short-range goals might change in their order of importance. By knowing this and being prepared to alter our course when necessary, we will always keep moving forward.

The following are points to always keep in mind:

1. A well-balanced person is one who is productive and constructive, but not to the point where he drives himself to destroying his body or mind. Goals should be diligently pursued, but without going to extremes that are self-destructive or cause artificial inspiration to be required. This is why goals must be realistic and attainable. You control your goals, *don't let them control you!*

2. Keep your body in vigorous physical condition. Practice a program of personal physical fitness. This is much more important than most people realize. Mental growth is boosted when the body is in its best shape.

3. Eat the right foods. Don't eat every meal as if it were your last.

The Living Dreamer

4. Make opportunities to be of service to someone every day. It is in treating others as you desire to be treated, that the best relationships are formed and previously unforeseen opportunities become available.
5. Express appreciation and kindness to others. The person who is interested in his or her associates, expressing appreciation for their services, will bring out the best in everyone.
6. Stay ahead of the game. Never become a straggler that soon falls into a pool of stagnation, where you will only be treading water. No one has ever achieved success by dragging his or her feet. There are three types of people in this respect: those who drag both feet (having no goals), those who drag one foot (goals are undefined), and those who stand on their own two feet, walk straight, and know where they are going, *because they planned it that way!*

Just as there are definite points to follow to attain success, there are also certain things which will hinder our progress:
- Insincerity;
- Dishonesty;
- Procrastination (no set time present in goal);
- Devotion to "fallacies" (ones which have no real meaning, superficial, or are not relevant to our purpose);
- Complacency;
- Loss of purpose;
- Nagging doubts concerning our ability to stick to our goals.

If it ever seems that you try again and again to bring your goals to fruition without success, remember—you are the inventor of the conditions in your life. *The goals that you are totally and wholeheartedly dedicated to will inevitably come into existence.*

Hold steadfastly to the successful manifestation of your goals. Refuse to be swayed by the false "opinion" of any lack or limitation that you have. Be determined to approach all tasks efficiently and confidently. Stay with your goals until they become a part of you.

Step II – Goals

There is magic in having goals for they have a way of breathing life into what seems impossible. Goals are essential for motivation and incentive. Motivation is the science of using every honorable means to challenge people to exert themselves toward a worthy purpose in life, using all of their abilities, experience and training.

No longer will you need to just imagine your life changing for the better. You are on your way to breaking away and standing out from the crowd. Being mediocre, when great things are possible, is one of the greatest tragedies that can befall any person.

All of us have the ability to bring our dreams, hopes and ambitions into the real world. And each individual has no competition in that realm. Anyone can know happiness, complete tasks of great significance, and make a meaningful contribution to others and to life.

Grab hold of life with a grip and tenacity of purpose that challenges you to accomplish your goals. You really desire to be great? Then believe it, work toward it, and *it will become a reality!*

As an individual thinks, believes and acts—so that individual becomes. So why not become great?! Our thoughts, faith, and actions, guided by our goals, will bring the ultimate satisfaction with the knowledge that we have succeeded in accomplishing what we have set out to do.

The Living Dreamer

I bargained with life a penny,
and life would pay no more.
However I begged at evening when I counted my scanty score.

For life is a just employer, it gives you what you ask.
But once you have set the wages,
Why, you must bear the task.

I worked for a menial's hire, only to learn, dismayed,
that any wage I had asked of life,
Life would have willingly paid."

— Jesse D. Rittenhouse

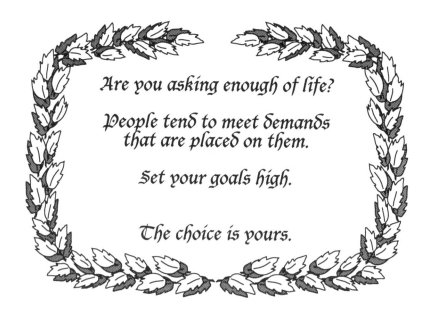

Are you asking enough of life?

People tend to meet demands
that are placed on them.

Set your goals high.

The choice is yours.

Step III
Silhouette of Success

It has already been discussed that a majority of the people have absolutely no idea of where they are going. They think in terms of generalities and have no plans. They will spend more time planning their vacation than they ever will planning their future. So many yearn for success, but only a few know what success really is.

If you were to conduct a survey of people on the street, only a handful could give you a competent definition of success. When asked, they would probably say it is wealth. Pictured by society in general, success is a pseudo-state of affluence. However, this does not represent the true meaning of success, for it is not necessarily of monetary value.

It can be stated that success is an awareness of the realization of one's goals. Success is a journey; it is not a destination. It is also a never-ending journey. When a person stops at the first sign of success, they will soon decline and become stagnant. They will finally cease to progress at all.

Success can be defined as the "progressive realization of a worthwhile purpose." Your worthwhile purpose is your ultimate achievement; and your goals are the progressive achievements necessary to attain your worthwhile purpose.

Success, therefore, becomes a progressive, continuous effort. It is not to be confused with mere achievement. *It is the more difficult feat of guiding your life efficiently to the realization of your definite purpose.* Success is actually an inside job. Deep within every person are the qualities for making his or her life a success. And until a person actually *feels successful*, they cannot *be successful*. Concentrate on your purpose, and you will draw out the necessary ingredients that will help you to feel successful, and become a success. You must make a decision on what you desire to do with your life, who you desire to be, and what you are willing to contribute in order to achieve this.

The Living Dreamer

Years ago, Russell Conwell raised millions of dollars for education with his famous speech, "Acres Of Diamonds." He told of an Arab who sold his farm and went on a world-wide search for diamonds, only to end his life by suicide; a poor, frustrated man. Meanwhile, the man who had bought the farm took his camel to a garden brook for water. As the animal drank, the man noticed a curious flash of light. From the white sands of the stream, he lifted a black stone with the light reflecting all the colors of the rainbow. The man had found a huge diamond! The stream was explored further—more diamonds everywhere!

This was the famous diamond mine of Golconda that was discovered. "Had Ali Hafed remained at home and dug in his own cellar," said the story teller, "he would have had 'acres of diamonds.' For every acre of that old farm, yes, every shovelful, afterward revealed gems which since have decorated the crowns of monarchs."

People underestimate their own great valuable property—*themselves.* We seem to think there is a pot of gold at the end of the rainbow, restlessly searching for riches in places where there are no riches. The real "gem of life" is the individual person. We should first try to mine and polish the value within ourselves. We have our individual identity, which is a possession much more valuable than diamonds.

So many times the treasure we seek is already ours, but we are blinded by the lure beyond to such a degree that we can't see the immediate value at home.

A California rancher, back in 1847, heard that gold had been discovered in Southern California. With a passion for gold, he sold his ranch to Colonel Sutter and away he went, never to return. Colonel Sutter put a mill upon a stream that ran through the ranch. One day his daughter brought some wet sand from the stream into the house and sifted it through her fingers. In that falling sand, a visitor saw the shining scales of real gold, the first that was ever discovered in California. The man who had owned the ranch desired gold, and he could have had it for the taking, right in his own back yard. Thirty-eight million dollars have been taken out of those few acres since then. Yes, $38,000,000!

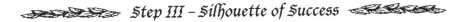

Step III – Silhouette of Success

Success does not come to the individual who only wishes for it. But it will come to the individual who decides that it will be his and works hard to make it happen. The only place that "success" ever comes before "work" is in the dictionary.

Financial success is not difficult to achieve in terms of competition. Only a few people are making an all-out effort to succeed. The competition will thin the higher you climb. The main difference in people who earn $25,000 and people who earn $5,000 a year *is the way they think.*

However, your greatest struggle will not be in climbing the ladder of success, but in getting through the crowd at the bottom. Well-meaning friends and relatives tend to judge us on their merits. When we can overcome their nonproductive thinking, that will be a great accomplishment in itself.

Whether they know it or not, every person has the responsibility to investigate and explore his or her own assets for success. One should always look for the resources close to home before trying to find them far away.

A farmer in Pennsylvania decided to sell his farm and secure employment collecting coal oil for his cousin in Canada. He wrote to his cousin, who answered in return, "I cannot employ you, because you know nothing about the oil business."

The farmer, determined to learn and with commendable zeal, set out to study the entire subject. He began with the second day of Nature's Creation, when the world was covered with that rich vegetation which has since turned into beds of coal. He studied it until he knew everything about coal oil—what it looked like, smelled like, tasted like, and how to refine it.

Writing his cousin again, he told him he now understood the oil business. His cousin wrote back stating that he had a position open. So the farmer sold his farm for $833 and departed for Canada.

After the new owner had taken possession of the farm, he went out to arrange for the watering of his cattle. He discovered that years before the previous owner had put a plank across the banks of the stream that ran behind the barn. The plank had sunk a few inches into the surface of the water, pushing a scum to the other bank, which the

The Living Dreamer

cattle would not put their noses in.

It was later found that this man who had traveled to Canada looking for coal oil had, for twenty-three years, been damming back a flood of oil which was declared by the state geologists to be worth a hundred million dollars—$100,000,000! This man had studied the subject of coal oil from the second day of creation up until the present time. Yet he failed to take the time to study the assets in "his own back yard." He sold his fortune for $833!

All of us have assets many times more powerful than we think, and all of these are available free of charge. It is up to each of us to utilize them. Not only for our own benefit, but also for the benefit of others.

We are born with everything we need to succeed. So it is up to us to understand and use what we already have. People often place limits on their success, but they never limit their degree of failure. It is time to reverse this procedure and get rid of the self-imposed limitations. When *we reverse our thinking we will reverse our direction.*

There are thousands of reasons to fail, but one does not need a reason to succeed. We owe it to ourselves to try. Can you overcome failure? You certainly can, *if you choose to believe you can!*

First, recognize where you have failed before. Now think of failures as part of the past. Think of them as a "polishing emery for your gem of success." Your fear of failure will vanish, for you will now see that these are very much a part of the process of success. Now, remember all of the times you have succeeded. Even if small, keep the memory of these times constantly before you.

Remember, it costs you more to be a failure than it does to become a success. A failure uses up just as much energy as does success. The successful person is the individual who stays on the job longer. A failure is a quitter.

Here is another simple exercise to practice: Each night before you go to sleep, visualize in your mind acting out your life as though you are already successful. See yourself in every single situation you can imagine, picture yourself doing exactly as you would with your goals materialized. Feel what it is like, and feel comfortable. Discuss, compromise and make decisions in this exercise. As you condition

Step III – Silhouette of Success

yourself in your mind, you will carry this over in real life, each day living the role you desire to play as though you had already succeeded and attained it.

This experience is invaluable and the results will amaze you. Soon you will become aware that you are no longer playing a role; success-thinking will become a habit. The mind cannot distinguish between the real and the imaginary. It takes the information you feed it and changes it to tangible reality. It actually will bring what you desire into being. But you must feel and act successful before success will reveal itself. You must believe and really desire something for this principle to work. *It will work when it is given the opportunity.*

Often, too much emphasis is placed on outward success rather than on the inner person. A truly successful individual is willing to share his or her knowledge and experience to help others achieve success. There is no room in their life for envy, greed, or thoughts of compensation. Successful individuals know happiness is one thing that will "multiply by division."

There is a law of retribution to remember and live by. It is called the "Circle Of Good"—when you do something good, it will always come back to you. It might not happen immediately, but happen it will! It cannot be denied you. A good act sets up a subconscious obligation, or automatic retention, that will be repaid with good. By helping someone else, you are automatically compensated.

It is also very important to practice the Golden Rule—"Do unto others as you would have them do unto you." When you treat all people how you would like to be treated—with love and accepting them in spite of their faults—their acceptance of you will follow in step.

Attitude/Motivation Concepts

Discover the most important word in the dictionary—Attitude. Your daily attitude not only determines your outlook on life, it determines the way the world looks at you. A proper attitude begins with confidence in yourself. Believe in yourself. Believe you can succeed, and you will.

The Living Dreamer

Practice a simple exercise of starting each day with anticipation instead of apprehension. Think of yourself as being reborn every day. When you begin each day with a new attitude, everything about life will change just by the way you look at it.

Having the right attitude is essential for us to keep striving towards our true potential; especially when situations don't turn out exactly as we'd like. It's our attitude that affects how we feel about ourselves, the way we look at life, and how we deal with the circumstances that life unexpectedly sends our way.

All of us have had to face something that we would rather just go away. Looking at these as situations rather than problems helps us to deal with them. If we feel better about taking care of something that needs our attention, we will be able to handle it easier and with a sense of accomplishment. So the next time you are facing something you don't want to, try to look at it as a challenge. Work through it. Don't run away from it. It will probably end up not being as hard as you first thought.

You can change your attitude by looking forward to the challenges. Practice attitude motivation—make it a daily exercise to motivate yourself. You will find everything so much easier to accomplish and accept. Life won't seem so much like a chore.

Sometimes it may feel like we are stuck in a rut. We may have developed a habit of being lazy, or perhaps are not feeling up to anything, thinking that this will soon pass and we'll be back on our feet. But it doesn't happen by just waking up one day with things being different. Things change in our life because *we make the effort to change it.* And once that first step is taken—the decision to want to—it will definitely be much easier than we imagined.

It's our how we think—our attitude- that makes the difference! And we are the only ones that have the power to make that change!

We can, at any given moment, change our outlook on life by altering our attitude. It is an immediate change and really so simple to do. A small change in our thinking can make a large impact on our sense of direction. Just take the time to try. Make an effort, maybe for the first time, and see the difference in your own life. After all, these are only words on paper and have no value until they are applied in a

Step III – Silhouette of Success

real sense. Your life will not change until you take these principles to heart and follow through on them.

Now that the ground work has been laid, you can develop the quality that is found in every successful man and woman, that slight edge that places them above the crowd. This quality is self-motivation. Your degree of success will be in direct proportion to your ability to motivate yourself.

First of all, what motivates people? Most simply conform to their environment. They are conditioned to accept things and themselves as they are, and not try to go any further. They accept the level of financial position of their friends, relatives and neighbors as suitable for their own. They feel it was just meant to be like this. Their success is limited by this same conformity. Life (for them) is not a challenge—it has become routine. It never enters their minds that even though they live in a nation of wealth and opportunity, they somehow cannot imagine it was ever meant for them. Their first job offers become their total life endeavors.

This need not be true for you. Begin to rise out of conformity. Remember, you owe it to yourself to try. Begin to think for yourself, think of your future, and use this concept of self-motivation to improve yourself daily. You need to decide what it is you are working toward. Are you motivated by what you desire? Have you even taken the time to decide what it is that you desire? Or are you being motivated by the masses?

Let's analyze the three basic types of motivation:

1. Fear Motivation: This is the first type of motivation we can remember. At an early age, we were most easily controlled by the fear of consequences. As an adult, we have found that motivation by fear is negative and short-lived. Therefore, it is the least effective.

2. Reward Motivation: The application of reward motivation is the opposite of fear motivation. People desire to achieve and will respond to reward motivation. However, this type of motivation is usually temporary, especially once the individual's needs are satisfied. Reward motivation also does not inspire people to utilize their full potential.

The Living Dreamer

3. Self-Motivation/Attitude Motivation: Since we are in direct control of our attitude, this type of motivation is lasting and worthwhile. A conscious daily effort is made to improve our attitude and to motivate our energy. We begin to notice the latent potential in ourselves (and in others) and begin to realize the abundant opportunity life has to offer. We become self-starters. We learn to control our thinking and to improve our daily attitude. Soon life takes on greater significance.

You will find that the only lasting and worthwhile motivation is self-motivation. This holds the key to your success as it is developed through your proper attitude towards life. Being able to "recharge" one's own motivating energies, without the help of any outside source, is the first and utmost quality of being a successful achiever.

An integral and closely related trait of success can be found in the wisdom and skill in keeping up the regenerating of self-motivation, in lieu of the constant outside pressure put on you. It is just as important to keep from being demotivated by others as it is to motivate yourself and other people.

If there are people in your life that bring you down, one way or another, then practice this simple exercise before retiring tonight: Create a mental scene of all those who might have, consciously or unconsciously, caused you to lose ground, or who constantly take the "wind out of your sail." You need to neutralize this effect on your thinking, and even more so, on your actions. (Take note: the statement is to "neutralize their effect." It may very well be that they are not even aware of their devastating effect on you! They are thinking in terms of the motiveless majority.)

In order to understand what exactly motivates you, then ask yourself this question: "Do I have to be motivated with an incentive or outside circumstances, or have I learned to generate my own motivation—to put ME in action?"

We can also motivate ourselves by a constant reminder of our burning desire to achieve our goals, and ultimately our worthwhile purpose. By thinking, feeling, and believing in them we will be setting

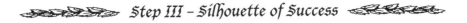

Step III – Silhouette of Success

ourselves on fire with motivation to achieve them! ***The full realization of our goals will be inevitable.***

You have only one life to live, so why not live your life to its fullest potential? Your success is not a measure of comparison or competition with others. It is your success; the progressive realization of your worthwhile purpose through achieving your goals. The only competition you have is with yourself. Continuous self-improvement through your own potential is growth and a major part of your success. Motivate yourself to purposeful action. Your success is up to you and no one else.

Alexander Graham Bell said, "Don't keep forever on the public road, going only where others have gone. Leave the beaten path occasionally and drive into the woods. You will be certain to find something you have never seen before. Follow it up. One discovery will lead to another, and before you know it, you will have something worth thinking about. All really big successes are the result of thought."

Remember—the beaten path is for beaten people!

Don't ever think that successful people are problem-free individuals, for no one is ever "free" from problems! You must try not to let yourself become demotivated by little situations. Try to be above this. A self-motivated individual learns how to effectively solve these everyday situations without being entrapped by doubt, worry or fear. Your future is based on the extent you use your mind. Control your thinking, motivate yourself, and success will be yours.

Success is the happiness derived in achieving your worthwhile purpose and goals. Success is continuous growth—growing from where you were to where you desire to be. You must become mentally successful before you can reap the real rewards of success. However, before success physically appears in reality, you must first render the service.

John Jacob Astor once had a mortgage on a millinery store which could not sell enough hats to pay the interest on his money. He foreclosed the mortgage, took possession of the store, and went into partnership with the very same people, in the same store, with the same capital. He gave them no more money. In order for the store to obtain money, they had to sell the merchandise.

He left the store and sat down on a bench in the park. He watched the ladies as they went by to see what kind of hats they were wearing. When a lady passed him with her shoulders and head erect, looking straight ahead as if she were proud of the clothes she was wearing, he studied her bonnet. By the time she was out of sight, he knew the shape of the bonnet's frame, the color of the trimmings and the crinkling of the feathers.

He went back to the millinery store, described the hat, and told them to make it and put it in the window. Back to the park bench he would go to resume his bonnet watching. The shop windows were soon filled with bonnets he knew the ladies liked. This was the foundation of the greatest store in New York with that line, and it still exists as one of three stores. Its fortune was made by John Astor after the business had failed, not by giving more money, but by finding out what the ladies liked before any material was wasted in making up the bonnets.

Now, let's study a law of success: our rewards in life are always equal to our service. What you put forth, you will get back in return. When you are dissatisfied with your position in life today, re-evaluate your contribution to it. Think of ways in which you can give more. You will then receive more.

Success can be quickly acquired when you write down your goals, think of them constantly, picture yourself achieving them, and then begin working towards their accomplishment.

Success requires action; action requires motivation. Motivation is goal-directed action. Motivate yourself permanently from within. Eliminate the application of fear or reward motivation. Practice attitude motivation. *Dedicate yourself to becoming successful.* Success is strictly and emphatically *up to you!*

In Bingham, Massachusetts, years ago there lived a man and his family. The man was out of work for some time and family relations were becoming strained due to his lack of income. One day he sat on the shore of the bay and whittled a soaked shingle into a wooden chain. That evening, his children quarreled over it and he whittled a second one to keep peace.

Step III - Silhouette of Success

While he was whittling the second one, a neighbor came by and said, "Why don't you whittle toys and sell them? You could make money at that."

The neighbor suggested the whittler should ask his own children what kind of toys to make. Acting on the hint, the next morning he asked his daughter, Mary, what kind of toys she would like. She named a doll's bed, a doll's washstand, a doll's carriage, and so on.

He had only had enough money for firewood, so he had no choice but to use it in order to make the toys. He began to sell them through the boot and shoe store next door. He made a little money, then a little more. Today this man is worth 100 million dollars—all from those strong, sturdy, unpainted Bingham toys that are now known all over the world. At thirty-four years of age he had made a fortune by applying the knowledge of what his own children liked to know what other children would like as well.

Always be alert for your opportunities wherever you are. They are waiting for your discovery. There is an expression, "being in the right place at the right time." Someone notices you; someone sees something special in you, or what you can do. It happens all of the time. *So strive for that "something" that makes you feel special!* Keep your eyes and ears open for the opportunities that seem to have "your name on them."

However, to be in *that place, at that time, for that opportunity,* it takes the inner knowledge of knowing what you want, and what direction you want to go with your life—**to be able to recognize the opportunity!** If you have no idea of what you want, or which direction you want to go, then how can you ever get any farther than where you are right now?

Obtain your ultimate success by living one day at a time. Live your best, and give your best. Make it a habit of succeeding by striving for success in everything you attempt. This is a big, wide, wonderful world we live in. Life has so much to offer that it need never be a bore. It should always be an exciting adventure. Learn to participate in all that life has to offer, and expect the best from life.

The Living Dreamer

One day a woman attended a meeting where the speaker challenged his audience to make the most of their every opportunity. When she went home and tried to take off her collar, the collar button stuck in the button hole. Disgusted with it, she said, "I am going to invent something better than that to put on collars." Her husband made fun of her, but she ignored him and went to work. She invented the snap button with a spring cap attached to the outer side. The button, which is used on many items of clothing, simply pushes together. To unbutton it, you simply pull it apart. She invented other buttons, and was taken into partnership by manufacturers. She gained a great fortune because she did not overlook the opportunity at hand, and ignored the laughter.

When you have the right mental attitude, it makes no difference what is going against you. Always turn situations to your advantage. Say "that's good" about every situation, and then get to work making good come out of it. You can be the master of your fate when you control your thinking. Don't let others think for you, do your own thinking. And never lose your capacity to enjoy life. You can't live yesterday and tomorrow. Live today, right now!

Not even one successful person ever started at the top. Remember, *success is the progressive realization of your worthwhile purpose—doing what you really desire to do.* Only a few successful people are doing so. The basic trouble today is conformity—to the wrong ideals. People who succeed today do so because they know where they are going. They have made plans. They have set goals.

Many people are afraid of success. Some are even uncomfortable with the idea. It is a foreign world where some of us feel like we don't belong. This is a common feeling at first. Usually, it is because we have been conditioned to believe that we are just "average individuals." This may have evolved from our immediate environment where we have lived (or are presently living), or from the mediocre, motiveless society. No matter what the reasons are, we have the capability and capacity to change how we think and feel about ourselves.

By removing this handicap we are taking a giant leap up the ladder of success. For us to be able to do this, *we have to change the way we think.* We must remove every single doubt, all negative thoughts

Step III – Silhouette of Success

and images that enter our mind and *we must do it every single time and at the exact moment that they present themselves!*

Next, replace these with positive thoughts and images, and do this every time. You are now controlling your thinking! The end result will be a sense of accomplishment instead of a defeated feeling, and you will be feeling this sense of accomplishment each time you do this.

As this experience is repeated over and over, it will be creating within you a relaxed sense of encouragement and enjoyment. As you practice this exercise in conjunction with the other simple exercises explained in this step, you will begin to feel at ease and secure with success. You will begin to feel very comfortable with your inner image of success. You are actually clearing the road for the inevitable success that will soon take place in your life.

It is also very important to associate with the right kinds of people—those with success on their minds and in their words and actions. Listen to those who desire and have what you also want in your life, and also to those who are earning the kind of money you desire to earn. These individuals can be excellent examples that our own efforts can be patterned after.

The opportunity is here and now. In the United States alone, more millionaires were "created" in the last few years than in its entire history.

The Living Dreamer

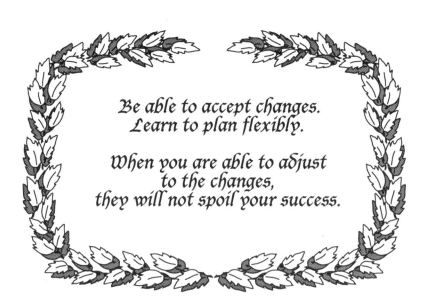

Be able to accept changes.
Learn to plan flexibly.

When you are able to adjust
to the changes,
they will not spoil your success.

Adventure II
The Principles of
The Living Dreamer

1. Only five percent of the working American population ever develop the right mental attitude. Set your goal to be in the top five percent of your co-workers.

2. You can become as successful as you *think you can.*

3. Do not wait until "everything is right" for you to become a success. You will no doubt be waiting for the rest of your life. Start right now.

4. Ninety-five percent of the people are "pre-conditioned." You need not be one of them. Believe you can succeed and you will.

5. Success comes to people who think productive. You can do anything that you can conceive in your mind—*but only when you believe it.* So begin by getting your mind in the right frame.

6. Act successful in your personality. Be enthusiastic and sure of yourself.

7. Get your energy "charged" by applying the attitude/motivation concepts.

8. Have the courage to take that first step—put action to work.

9. Handle each of life's situations one at a time. Don't worry about it, just handle it.

10. Don't depend on anyone else for your success—they might even be depending on you!

The Living Dreamer

11. Use the qualities that you possess efficiently and wholeheartedly.

12. Relax and listen—sometimes you just might learn something.

13. Define and set your goals. How much more do you desire to earn than what it takes to merely survive?

14. Learn the art of constructive investing. You don't necessarily need money to earn money.

15. Do not fear failure. You will only have to be right fifty-one percent of the time to be right.

16. Make yourself happy—decide to be.

17. Sell yourself, but don't sell yourself short.

18. Learn to understand other people by observing them. They will no doubt be judging you on their merits. And don't get "locked into" a crowd of those who don't know where they are going.

19. People are basically honest, productive, good individuals.

20. Love all people with a total understanding of unity. When you learn to accept their faults, they will accept yours.

21. Whenever you are in doubt about anything—do not pass judgment.

22. Don't violate the rights of others. Use common sense and treat others with respect.

23. One individual, together with one other person, is a team at work. Team members should believe in each other, support and encourage each other.

24. Read books that are constructive and productive.

25. Always tell the truth. You are worthy, but only as worthy as you think you are.

26. Be in control of your thoughts. Think for yourself.

Adventure II – Principles

Your Special Clues for Success:

Daydreaming
utilizing
Pictorialization
and
Visualization
by activating the
Imagination

Utilize these special clues for success. You will find that success is progressive. Dare to create new experiences, and you will create greater successes that are born in thought.

The success power of image-fixing is so important that you will find it constantly mentioned in many beautiful success stories everywhere. Imagination is a well known art and an ancient technique for success.

Picture a daydream and watch that daydream come true, in its own time.

Nature shows you a phenomenon of light: it is the darkest just before the dawn. Life is persistent to your success ideas. The resistance is the greatest just before the dawn of success.

Maintain the persistence of thoughts in success attitude, and the dawn of success will enter into your life.

When it seems your success is being withheld from you after you have worked very hard to achieve success:

Instead of trying to reason with people, or try to explain to people why you have not yet achieved success, quietly get busy in your mind picturing the images of the end-results you desire. The images you create that have a time-concept in this picture (these events need to "know" when they are to happen) will then be able to take place. Learn to use the picture power of your mind to keep focused on your long-range goals, as you enjoy your everyday life and its pleasures.

47

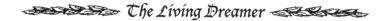

Remember the "Triple 'A' Motto":

Attitude: This is a way of thinking. When you have a positive thought you cannot have a nonproductive one at the exact same time.

Altitude: Success requires a certain degree of excitement.

Action: This is the catalyst that creates productive and constructive thoughts that will produce the results.

$$A = A = A$$

Adventure II – Principles

Use this Simple Formula for Success:

Develop a burning desire.
Provide the necessary action.
You will achieve the degree of
success you desire.

Desire plus Action equals Success ($D + A = S$).

"Success is . . ."

Success is the continuous organization of opportunity, ability, and time.

Success is the enjoyment of the journey and not some magic point in a successful career.

Success is love in action blended with the environment.

Success is the mind expressing itself in simplicity.

Success is time. Time is given to each and every one of us to create what we desire. What is it that we desire in life? What lifestyle will give us the things we desire for our loved ones?

Success answers the age-old question, "How?" By organizing the thoughts in our mind to create a world for the future; and to use the past only as a reference to permeate forward, with progress.

Success is attitude. The thoughts we create are the end-result of our mind and its language.

Success is a "law of the mind." (Just as gravity is a law of the same kind of unseen force.)

Success comes to the individual with a successful self-image. (The mirror will reflect the image which is shown to its environment.)

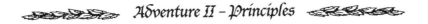# Adventure II - Principles

"What am I...Success"

"You will desire to know me for exactly what I am, because you have selected me for an integral part of your life. Your future happiness depends largely upon how thoroughly you become familiar with all the facets of my past and present existence. You will find that what I have to say to you and what I have to show you is interesting and thrilling. So come with me while I tell you my story. It is an autobiography, a kind of psychological character study, because what I am today has developed out of my environment and can be traced to experiences in my youth. Although I am reaching out for perfection, I have already done very well. I have made mistakes. I am stronger and better for them.

I was born of necessity, created by modern civilization. I have been nourished by the growing complexities of life and earning a living. I am today spreading across the continent and the world with increasing momentum and greater strides than ever before. My growth, my strength, and my speed have never been matched in the history of Man or Woman. You will find me in concentrated industrial areas. You will find me in rural communities. You will find me in cities working with retailers in their stores, in offices both large and small. I am in the world among the one-person businesses, among proprietors, superintendents and marketing people. I am the friend of professional men and woman alike. Doctors, lawyers, dentists, and too many to list. I am welcomed by newspaper writers, advertising people, and artists. I stabilize the economy of communities throughout the world. Merchants, food stores, drug stores, and all business owners share in my wide spread benefits. I seem to be everywhere.

The Living Dreamer

Where I am, peace of mind spreads. You will find me in the hearts of smiling fathers. You will find me giving strength to those who work. You will know I am present when you hear the happy shouts of children home from school, greeting their parent who is waiting for them. There is no doubt where I stride. I am healthy because I travel in good company. I radiate happiness because I perform great social services. Yet, beneath my happy exterior lies much concern. For throughout, I am needed in many more places. I cannot go there because I am not invited, although I am generally welcomed. Some misunderstand me and shut their hearts and their minds to me. Even though I help many millions, I need the help of many thousands in carrying out my duties. I have long been on the Earth, though it is in comparatively recent years that. I have grown so rapidly to my present lustrous stature. No one dares predict how great my future is, but all agree on this: 'It is tremendous. I do this humbly, aware of my role in life and my heavy responsibilities. For I am success…'"

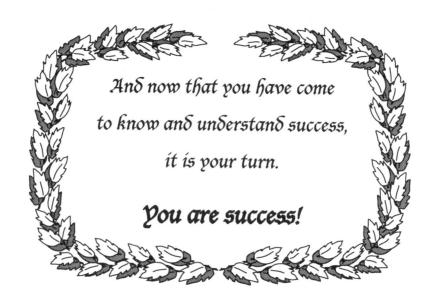

And now that you have come to know and understand success, it is your turn.

You are success!

Step IV
Desire

How Badly Do You Want Something?

You may often hear people say, "I want this," and "I want that." Perhaps you have even made these statements yourself. However, nothing ever seems to materialize. You really have to wonder just how badly something is wanted. Is it just a whim? Is it just a passing fancy? How do you know how badly you really want something?

Once there was a wise old man who had one of his students ask him, "Wise teacher, will you teach me what I must do to attain success?"

The wise, old teacher waded out into the water up to his chest and told the young man to come out to him.

The young man, obeying, walked out into the water to his master. The teacher, being much bigger and stronger than the young student, grabbed him when he got within his reach and shoved the young student's body, head and all, under the water and held him under the water.

The wise teacher kept him there, and he struggled and struggled to get to the top of the water for a breath of air. The teacher held him under the water until he quit struggling and went limp from exhaustion and lack of oxygen. The wise teacher then lifted him up out of the water and let the young student gasp and gasp for air, and let his lungs fill with oxygen.

Finally, the young man said, screaming, "What is the matter with you old man! Are you trying to drown me?!"

The teacher gently carried the young student to the bank of the river, and asked, "What was the one thing that you wanted most as I held you under the water?"

The Living Dreamer

Gasping for a breath, he screamed at the old man, "I wanted to breathe, you old fool! I wanted to breathe!"

The wise man said, "Young man, when you want success as bad as you wanted to breathe when I held you under the water, then, and only then, will you attain the success in life that you want."

Desire is a longing for an object or an experience which promises satisfaction in its attainment. If you really want to achieve your goals, your worthwhile purpose, and be successful, you must begin with a burning desire. It is one of the most effective motivating factors known to humankind. Without this burning desire, nothing of consequence will ever be achieved.

Comparatively few will ever realize the importance of a burning desire. The world is full of people wallowing in negativism and nonproductiveness. They do not take the time to realize that it is just as easy to be a success as it is to be a failure. Most of them are content to accept their positions in life without ever raising their sights to higher pinnacles. They are vaguely dissatisfied and have nebulous dreams about what they might otherwise be doing—only nothing ever materializes.

These dreams never become realities because there is no "force" behind them. Dreams remain just that—dreams. A majority of the people think of dreaming as a pastime for adolescents. This is not the truth of the matter. Everything worthwhile that is ever accomplished has been done by people who are dreamers with faith in their dreams.

These dreamers have something strong going for them, and it works magically to turn their dreams into living realities. That something is their *burning desire.*

Burning desire is the emotional force that arouses the creative power of the mind to bring you the object of your desires. This is the power that makes the impossible possible. It is the driving force of destiny.

How do we "switch on" a burning desire? We revive our childlike desire to learn.

Approximately one-half of the knowledge we possess has been learned by the age of ten. A child of five can absorb three hundred new bits of information a day, while the average adult will usually limit

Step IV – Desire

themselves to about twelve new bits of information in one day. Children learn twenty-five times more a day than adults, *simply because they are interested.*

Do you remember from your childhood how pleasant the sensation is to sit in the top of a tree and look down on the rest of the world.

One man who had enjoyed climbing a tree when he was a young boy used his foot to step on the moon. Impossible? So it had seemed at one time. Accomplished? Indeed! Now he truly views the earth—all of it—because as a boy he dreamed from the top of a tree, and he believed. As a man he dared his dream and achieved it. His name is Neil Armstrong, the first man to walk on the surface of the moon.

If you are saying to yourself, "I can't dream," then think again, because you can. Believe something great is coming your way and get ready to receive it. You can do whatever it is that you desire and can become a great person in your own unique way. Remind yourself that your complete mental picture is in proportion to your potential—not someone else's potential—and your own perseverance.

You are a very unique individual, and no one else possesses all of the qualities, capabilities, and ideas that are your own. What had seemed so far out of reach before you started reading this book will now seem quite possible. So dare to wake up and make your big dreams come true. You are now at a level of self-confidence that allows you to have goals with the belief that they will happen.

Once you have decided what you desire out of life and what you are willing to contribute to get it, your achievements are inevitable. You will discover your thoughts and actions will be focused on accomplishing your desires.

Perhaps you have been held back from your place in life by feeling that you are not as capable as others. What you become and what you achieve is not due to your natural ability and creative capacity alone. Although these are powerful assets, the greatest motivators are desire, and "stickability" (Step X). People who dream big, have a burning desire, a great drive for achieving and never give up, become their dream.

55

The Living Dreamer

All the inner qualities for true success grow from a burning desire. Desire is the beginning of all achievements. But you must keep your desire a burning and growing one for the road to success is always under construction.

Consider the following basic desires of humankind. How these desires fit into your life depends on your personality and individual "make-up." How they are dealt with determines your health, happiness, your place in life and your usefulness to yourself and to others.

1. The desire for security.

Individuals reared in an insecure environment often show the results of this background when they are adults. They commonly strive for prestige and financial gain to stifle the fears they have of being returned to their former insecure positions. Only those who realize the need to examine the past with its emotional trauma overcome these compulsive compensations. These people then become aware that material gains do not necessarily bring security. With this awareness, they can seek inner resources which lead to a more mature outlook. They begin to change from the love of things to a love of people. They also begin to experience good feelings of being related to people rather than having a life that is solely made up of "things."

2. The desire for success.

The desire to attain personal success is a basic drive in all people. There is a deep satisfaction in success. It is a strong motivation in healthy human beings. This had been thought of as being the basic desire only in men, but it is just as true for women. Women executives, for instance, are becoming more and more prominent in the business world along with their prominence in the community, social circles and the home.

You will succeed in any venture you truly desire to succeed in. When you do not succeed, your desires are simply ill-defined. Walter B. Pitkin, author of "The Psychology Of Achievement," says thousands of people can double, triple, and quadruple their

56

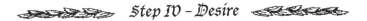 Step IV - Desire

effectiveness simply by being aroused to "creative audacity." So many lack courage for this, but it is only because they have not as yet turned on their desire, which releases the immense energies that are absolutely necessary in order to succeed.
3. The desire to be accepted.
   People want to be accepted. They will usually desire to become members of the "in-group." This will determine their behavior, their attire, their speech and their activities.
   Some young people will even become sexually promiscuous, experiment with drugs, rebel against their parents' teachings, often against their own better judgment. Some will go so far as to break the law in order to conform to their group's standards.
   Adults are sometimes just as guilty of this as the younger set. Some will sacrifice almost any belief or principle rather than take the chance of standing alone and being rejected for their convictions. When they do not feel like they are a part of a group, they have a sense of inferiority. When the reasons for this feeling of inferiority are not understood, extreme behavior is sometimes used to attract attention.
   Often an obsessive desire for acceptance has been brought on by a rejection suffered in the past. This is much more prevalent than you might think. These people fight against the very thing they long for—acceptance. In their fear of rejection, they reject others first. People have to accept themselves before they can accept others. Mature people recognize they have value and worth and accept themselves. However, most of the time people try too hard. All we really need to do is be ourselves.
4. The desire to be appreciated.
   This is one of the most unusual motivating forces in life. It requires so little effort, and yet the results are immeasurable. Workers will double their efforts when their employer speaks a few words of appreciation. A wife glows when her husband praises her. The feeling of being needed and valued increases in a man when his wife and children thank him for his hard work. One of the greatest joys in life for parents comes when their adult children express gratitude for their upbringing.

The Living Dreamer

People have a deep longing to be appreciated and desired. Appreciation will grow from the sense of gratitude for what has taken place in life. Ingratitude, an unbecoming trait, arises when people feel they owe no one for what they have—even though no person ever lives unto himself and dies unto himself.

The psychologist William James believed appreciation was the deepest longing of the human heart. Gratitude not only brings happiness to the one to whom it is expressed, it brings joy to the person expressing it. It adds depth to that person's character. A "little" person is incapable of appreciation. A "big" person is filled with a sense of gratitude.

5. The desire to be understood.

Our lives are astronomically enriched when we find someone who cares for and understands us, and who demonstrates this by being a good friend who is always ready to listen and help.

A major fault with many people is that they have stopped listening long before the other person has ceased talking. They tend to turn people on and off as they do their television sets. Anytime you refuse to listen, you have prejudged the other person's conversation by thinking their words are not worthy of your attention.

Individuals with sensitive natures often leads lonely lives because they feel no one understands them, even within their own family. The family relationship must be based on love and a desire to understand. One solution to a better understanding is through the art of listening; not only to the words being spoken, but especially to what the words are meant to convey. Develop the habit of listening between the words in the same way you might read between the lines of printed matter.

Understanding forms a "friendship circle" within human relationships. You must understand yourself before you can understand others. And it is in understanding others that you will gain more insight into yourself. Any person is indeed fortunate when he or she finds someone to trust who is understanding and worthy of that trust.

6. The desire to love and be loved.

It has been said that "the world is dying for lack of love." Why is this? One of the reasons is that most people have such a

Step IV - Desire

shallow and superficial concept of love. They have experienced little evidence of the "real thing" in their lives.

Genuine love can be exemplified in the thought, "What can I do to make you happy?" rather than, "What will you do to make me happy?" Giving love is actually more important than receiving it. It is also true that the more love we give, the more we will receive.

When people are willing to completely give of themselves to bring happiness and joy to one another, they can realize the depths of the love that is possible for them. True love involves a unity and an understanding of one's total self and being. When people know who they are, they can better give all that they are capable of.

7. The desire for a meaningful life.

This has been found to be a definite and worthwhile purpose of most people.

During World War II, Dr. Viktor Frankl, an Austrian psychiatrist, was a prisoner and lived through the horrors of a Nazi concentration camp. He noted that only those prisoners who had a defiant spirit and had found a "meaning for life" were able to survive!

The person who knows the "why" of living can bear the "how" of living. A meaningful life involves recognizing who we are and who we desire to become. It involves the love and acceptance of self, welcoming love from others, and sometimes even suffering with others—which is often the price one pays for being a member of the human race.

A person's attitude and spirit towards suffering reveals his or her outlook on life. But suffering does not have a real meaning unless it is absolutely necessary. And it is often only in reflection that we are able to see the lessons learned in our suffering.

It is imperative to establish a meaning for our lives. No life is ever "pointless." But if a person does not establish a reason for being, then life itself will seem unworthy of the time. Being the best that we can be is an excellent way of discovering a meaning for our lives.

These are some of the innate desires of every human heart. It is up to us to cultivate the proper incentive to carry these desires to their highest fulfillment.

The Living Dreamer

During your high school days, you probably witnessed athletes who "came into their own" on the playing field. Latent abilities were realized as a result of the stress in the game, the cheer from the crowd, and the desire to win. Desire demands! It is very powerful. But the cheering crowd is soon gone, and life's stresses increase. Individuals must learn to evaluate their desires. What was easy to accomplish on the playing field is not quite the same in the world outside of high school.

Burning desire provides the energy to move through your bondages of the past. Everyone has barriers built up because of nonproductive, negative-thinking people in their lives who have convinced them that they cannot achieve. Plant the following seeds of thought, feel them with conviction and confidence, and sow them in your mind, right now, concerning your own success:

- I am success.
- I have a meaningful life.
- I overcome fear and worry.
- I understand myself and other people.
- I am a healthy and happy person.
- I pull the curtain down on my past and burn my weak bridges.
- I am a "changer" of society and its handicaps.

Burning desire can help break down any of these barriers that stand in your way of progress. No matter which category your burning desire falls in, you can achieve it when you know what it is. The first step in getting it, however, is getting it clearly defined.

Many people engage in wishful thinking and daydreams, but idle daydreams wither and die from the lack of nourishment. These same daydreams, when taken out of the "idle" category, could be turned into realities when all fear and doubts are removed, and a strong belief in them is substituted instead.

So if you have a dream you have been dreaming of for years, that special something you have always desired and never believed you could have, there are a few rules for making it come true. But first, examine yourself on the following questions:

- Is it really what I desire to do?
- Is it really what I desire to be?

60

Step IV - Desire

- Is it really where I desire to go?
- Is this really what I desire to accomplish with my life?
- Am I willing to pay the price required to get it?
- **Is it realistic?** This is important. You cannot hope to be the first man or woman to land on Mars when you failed in science and mathematics and get airsick on an airplane, can you? Unless, of course, *you learned how to master them.*

After you have clearly defined your burning desire and know exactly what it is, and can single-point focus (Step II) and concentrate on what it is you desire, you must expend a great deal of extra effort in the following ways:

1. Mentally accept it pictorially—"video-visualize" it.

   Don't ever allow yourself to think about being unworthy of it. You are a unique individual. There is only one of you on this earth. When your desire is a worthy one, then you are worthy to receive it. *Accept it as your own and tell yourself several times a day that you deserve it and that you are going to get it.*

2. Visualize it coming to you with your imagination (picture screen or picture chamber) in your mind.

   Every time you think about it (and you must think of it constantly) picture it in your mind as being on its way to you—always traveling, through time and space, to land on your "doorstep."

3. Eliminate all nonproductive thoughts, doubts, and fears.

   Doubt and fear have no place in your life from here on! Tell yourself your desire is on its way and *you are going to have it!*

   Each time a doubt wanders in, "slam the door" to your mind and don't let it in! Destroy and pull it apart with a productive thought. Remember, you don't have to know the "whys and wherefores" of how you will achieve what you so ardently desire. This will all be unfolded for you. So put away all doubt, fear and hesitation.

4. Start believing and acting as though it has already happened.

   Picture in your mind how you are going to act and feel when your desire is achieved. Think about it, daydream about it, and start acting and feeling as if it is already yours, right now. This is the dress rehearsal for the real thing.

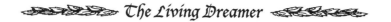 *The Living Dreamer*

5. Write it down.

Put your desire into a few words or make up a code word which you can identify with instantly in your mind with your desire. Write it down on several cards. Tape them to the mirror you use in the morning as you begin your day, on your car dashboard—and anywhere that you will see it several times a day. Keep a card in your pocket or purse and take it out often during the day and read it. While you are reading it, tell yourself your desire is already on its way to you.

6. Fall in love with it.

Remember when you fell in love with the one who is now your mate, or that special person you wanted in your life? This was that special one out of all the others you had to have. This person was different. As an individual, you were consumed and obsessed by the desire to make that person as yours; so much so that you put all your time and energies into making them yours. You thought about them, dreamed of them, and wooed them with all of your creative energies. This is the same thing you must now do for your desire. Fall in love with it with all of your power and might, and make it yours!

When you are into this program of achieving your desire and following all these rules laid out for you, you will be amazed at the things that will start happening in your life. Ways and means of attaining this desire will start revealing themselves. You will begin meeting people who will help you toward your goals. A casual word in a conversation will turn into an opportunity to push you further ahead on the road. Cooperation from others will be made available to you; opportunities you never expected will be presented. Your capacity to handle any situation will be enlarged.

This is all part of the magic that happens when you establish your purpose, outline your goals, and envision your desire.

Some thoughts that will inspire you to continue your climb up to success and let the desire within bring your creative forces into being:

- There is a world of wealth waiting for those who will claim it.

Step IV - Desire

- There is a productive and constructive power for those who are ready to exercise it.
- There is real success for those who seek to attain it.
- There is true happiness for those who are willing to share it.
- There is full meaning for those who are willing to find it.
- There is advancement and progress for those who are willing to achieve them.
- There are great days ahead for anyone filled with a desire!

When your purpose is inspired by desire it will accomplish these three great joys for you:
1. Your life will take on added dimensions;
2. Every home will be strengthened with more happiness;
3. Every business becomes more successful and more productive when its leadership absorbs a good dose of desire.

Desire draws out your natural abilities to their greatest potential. It grows in proportion to its freedom and use.

Whatever stage of success you are in, imagine yourself more successful and let your desire move you on and up. Associate with those applying the best to their lives and you will learn from them how to cultivate the best within yourself. Successful people keep their desires just as exciting even after their potentiality period. Desire reminds you that you can achieve and it also goads you to keep moving. It constantly tells us—You can do it! You can be great!

Remember there is no limitation to your abilities, for the real competition is only with yourself.

Make these your guidelines as you continue to climb in this Success Concept:
1. Determine your purpose.
2. Set your goals.
3. Plan your work and work your plan.
4. "Fan your flame of desire" to its fullest.
5. Do not accept criticism or suggestions from someone who is going to plant weeds in your mental garden.

The Living Dreamer

Desire is childlike in its simplicity, yet it is as complex as the mind of humankind. What is it in infants that makes them reach and be willing to reach again? It is the need to fulfill a desire. They are "designed" to love and be loved, placed in the cradle of security and acceptance, and directed through understanding toward success. Appreciated even in the lesser moments of greatness, they ultimately find their lives meaningful.

Desire? *Yes. We are made that way.*

Your purpose is your launch pad, your goal is your missile, and your desire is your fuel. Fire it up and take off! You, too, can reach the stars.

And you can do it!!

Step V
Self-Image

Do You Like the Image in the Mirror?

Do you remember the classical Biblical story of David and Goliath? Here we are presented with two unique individuals confronting each other in the battle of life. Goliath was a giant of a man, over seven feet of pure image, colorful cloth and shiny weapons. Facing him was a young, fragile, and barely clothed youth, with no image to speak of, and no glittering armor. But what he did have was a giant of a Self! A self overpowering all obstacles and handicaps, and the self that won him a name in human history.

For you to win the pearls and diamonds of life, you must cultivate your own self-image. Only when your image reflects a true and confident person, will you have the real self-image needed to earn you a place in the Hall of Success.

You have indicated your desire for self-improvement by becoming an adventurer and seeker of success. You may not have realized it, but every person has an unfavorable self-image until they participate in something successful. You form your own self-image in your mind and usually it is much too low.

Everyone can improve his or her self-image, and the quicker the better! One of our major goals in this Adventure of Success is to help you build your own self-image to an all-time high!

An important tool in the changing of one's self image is attaining the ability to make one's own decisions. Too many people tend to "lollygag" around when it comes to making a decision, and often the opportunity is lost.

The Living Dreamer

There is a story about a nineteen-year-old girl reared in the back-woods of South Carolina. She weighed about two hundred and fifty pounds and was as strong as a mule. She applied for and received a job on a farm close to town, so that she could see how the city people lived.

The owner of the farm sent her out to fix all the fences, thinking it would take her about a week to complete the job. In about half a day, she had finished. Next, she was to chop several acres of cotton. Again the job was completed in half a day.

The farmer was very happy with his new helper. He asked the girl to bring in ten tons of hay. This job was also done in half a day. Since all the chores were caught up, the farmer's wife asked when she could use her to separate potatoes. She took her to the cellar and told her to put the small potatoes in one pile, the middle-sized ones in another, and the large ones in still another.

When she returned after half a day, the girl was sitting in utter dejection. Not a single potato was moved. The farmer's wife asked, "What's the matter, Jean? How come you don't have the 'taters in them piles?"

The girl replied, "I don't mind working all you desire, but these decisions get me down."

It seems many people are like this. In order to attain a good self-image, you will have to be able to make decisions. Making decisions will pave the way for a better attitude towards yourself, and consequently greater self-appreciation.

Our self-image not only reveals how we feel about ourselves, it motivates our attitude towards others, and our actions and reactions to opportunities. To have "good" reactions, we need to feel good about ourselves. We need to love ourselves.

Too often, some of us may be like the little boy reared in a children's home. He became so depressed and unhappy, he ran away. After a long search, he was found on a factory roof, hiding behind a barrel. When asked why he had run away, he replied, "I'm nobody's nothing." This reflects the kind of attitude so many people have toward themselves. To be successful and happy, you must learn to be "somebody's something," and have a good self-image.

Step V - Self-Image

One of the greatest statements in the Bible is, "Thou shalt love thy neighbor as thyself." Loving ourselves means accepting ourselves as we are— but most of all, with an appreciation for the goodness within us. It also means realizing our faults *without* self-hatred; and to be willing to work on changing them. Only when we love and respect ourselves can we love and respect others.

Believe in yourself, improve yourself, develop your worthwhile purpose, and you will be delighted when life takes on more meaning, and you begin to realize a happiness you never knew existed.

You have so far used only a small part of your potential. Additional accomplishments, joy, and satisfaction are in store for you when you have the will to believe.

The eminent psychologist, William James, stated: "Compared to what we ought to be, we are making use of only a small part of our physical and mental resources. Stating the thing broadly, the human individuals that live far within their limits possess powers of various sorts which they habitually fail to use."

Timidity is often the enemy to a better self-image and ultimately, to the individual's success. It is best not to be too reluctant about our actions.

Ralph Waldo Emerson gives the perfect antidote to such a handicap: "Do not be too timid and squeamish about your actions. All life is an experiment. The more experiments you make the better. What if they are a little coarse and you may get your coat soiled or torn? What if you fail, and get fairly rolled in the dirt once or twice? Up again, you shall never be so afraid of a tumble."

So think of life like an experiment, and the more experiments you have the better off you are. Because when we have gone through something once, we won't be afraid the next time it comes around.

It is also very wise not to think of the experiences we go through as being either good or bad. It is actually from the so-called bad experiences that we learn the most about ourselves and others. So these experiences actually end up being very good for us to have!

Maybe you are one of many who sell themselves short on their real ability. If so, then prepare yourself for some big changes. In learning to develop success characteristics, there is someone you need to know extremely well. You have known this person all of your life.

67

The Living Dreamer

However, you may not have taken the time to study him or her very carefully. Perhaps you don't even understand this person at all. This person is you!

The failure to understand ourselves and to be ourselves is a weakness to overcome. Too many people are acting roles, trying to be someone else, someone they can't be! No one likes a pretender. These people obviously do not believe in themselves or in what they do and say. They are so busy trying to be someone else that they never take the time to analyze themselves, decide on who they are or what they believe in. They fail to be honest with themselves. No wonder they do not succeed! They have no foundation on which to build their lives. Too many years are wasted by trying (impossibly!) to fulfill another's destiny, and they never fulfill their own.

You have your own destiny. Most importantly, now you will be able to fulfill it.

So take some time right now to analyze yourself. Picture yourself, and ask:

- Do I like what I see?
- What do I like about myself?
- What don't I like?
- Do I know where I am going?
- What are my beliefs?

Taking time to study yourself is very important. After all, you are the most important person in the world, regardless of what you think, have been taught, or have been told. You hold the key to your future, and you are in the "driver's seat" of the most amazing devices known— the human mind.

The world today is aglow with space conversation—the Moon, Mars, and all of the galaxies beyond. Yet, the mind that triggers these thoughts has as much unexplored space and depth as the distance to any star. The mind is energy—lots of energy. For example, there is enough electrical energy in one human mind to light the entire city of Los Angeles for years, and enough creative force to keep many businesses busy for generations.

Step V - Self-Image

You have only been scraping at the surface instead of scooping up the tremendous potential of your mind. Only you can unlock the hidden potential within, direct your thoughts, control your life, and complete your worthwhile purpose.

To all this potential power there are certain keys, and only these keys will open the vast unexplored space known as the M-I-N-D. We cannot use the building blocks of life without following certain laws from within, before these can materialize on the outside.

You have the ability. Begin to believe in its existence. Then seek to improve and develop your own P-O-W-E-R. What you believe within yourself is what others will see in you. Believe there is weakness, timidity, and no real purpose, and that's exactly what others will believe about you.

When you are not progressing, maybe it's because you do not feel worthy. If this is the case, you must improve your "reflection." Put more into life. You can develop an image of yourself that is worth living up to. And then, put that "new self" into action. You, too, will soon be saying, "What a great life!"

Develop the power of your will, Mr. and Ms. Dynamite, and you will explode on the "Meteoric Sky of Life" as a great light, as energy, as one who has started the journey to the stars!

Part of your "fuel" is a clear, precise, truthful self-image. You are like a glass bottle. People can see right through you. The truth is in your eyes. All of the best relationships begin with an eye-to-eye encounter. If you can't look someone in the eyes, correct whatever it is within you that hinders this.

You have an opinion of yourself whether you spend a lot of time thinking about it or not. Think of your self-image as sort of jigsaw puzzle, a picture-puzzle-piece map that you consult about yourself regading who you are.

Now it is time for you to do a simple exercise. Go to a mirror, stand in front of it, and look at the image of yourself that's before you. That's right. Take a good, long look at who is staring back at you in the mirror. That's you. This is the person that you will have to live with for all of your life. *So learn to love this person!* Take care of this person,

The Living Dreamer

for this is the only thing that keeps you "fastened" to yourself. You are the only one who looks exactly like what you see reflected before you.

Now, maintain eye contact with the reflected image, *and don't lower your eyes!* Stare right into the center of the eyes. Now, step back and look at the image from head to toe. Firmly impress upon yourself (without judging) this image staring back at you.

Close your eyes now and see if you can still see or sense a picture, or image, of the one who is in the mirror. This image needs to be engraved on the screen of your mind, or picture chamber.

You must always remember that whoever is in the mirror staring back at you, is you—physically, your body—that you must live in for the rest of your life. It is your own self-image "world" within yourself, displayed to the outside world. No one else is within except you, and your image. So keep good note of that.

It is not important, at the present time, whether you like or dislike what you see or sense in the mirror. It is important that when you test yourself, by closing your eyes, that the image is still present on the picture chamber of your mind of who you saw in the mirror. Also, that you can recall this image to the attention of your mind at any time you so desire. Mind and body need to know who you are. An image, or a picture, is necessary to do this. Picture the image there, and keep it there. This way the "inner" you will know who it is that is instructing, whenever you are doing whatever to whomever.

Keep searching inside for anything else that robs you of the self-confidence that is needed to be able to meet others with assurance and expectancy. Go ahead, peek inside! Perhaps you have never done this before. If you find something that is a little disturbing, you will need to remove the "disturbance." Remember, there is always something to be improved—in everyone!

Individuals desire to be understood and to be accepted. Therefore, it is important to study and to understand yourself. You will find that your description of other people is actually a picture of yourself. There is no way to have a wholesome attitude about other people without first having a healthy attitude about yourself, and understanding yourself. Be yourself, and make it possible for others to accept you.

Step V – Self-Image

In your self-improvement, you need to search deep into your past and into your childhood. In what kind of environment were you raised? Remember, when people are at the early stages of their development, they are largely a product of their environment. This will reveal why you act as you do, and should cause you to question your actions as to whether they are for your good and productivity, and also for the best interest of all.

Part of this Adventure To Success is to help you unravel your past and to be free of its handicaps. Then, and only then, can you be yourself—a person you can admire and respect. You can't expect others to respect you if you do not respect yourself. No one can afford the consequences of a "warped" life. Maybe you need to sit down and prepare a "Ben Franklin Balance Sheet."

Americans have long considered Benjamin Franklin one of the wisest of men. Whenever this great patriot found himself in a situation such as you are in today, he felt pretty much as you do. When it was the right thing to do, he wanted to do it. When it was the wrong thing, he wanted to avoid it. Is this the way you feel?

Here is what Ben used to do. He would take a sheet of plain, white piece of paper, and draw a line down the middle. On the left side he would write "Yes," and on the right side he would write "No." Then he would evaluate himself according to certain characteristics.

Whether or not you have them, you may evaluate yourself by writing down the following qualities as a guide. Add more that you feel are important for you.

Integrity	Good Judgment	Courtesy
Honesty	Patience	Ambition
Enthusiasm	Consideration	Tolerance
Temperance	Friendliness	Creativity
Persistence	Gratitude	Humility
Aggressiveness	Humor	Tact
Appreciation	Imagination	Decisiveness
Understanding	Trustworthiness	Courage
Optimism	Loyalty	Assertiveness

The Living Dreamer

Evaluation is the beginning of progress. Strive to improve on the qualities listed on the "No" side, and be proud of the qualities on the "Yes" side. *All of us have been created to live our dreams!*

Seven Steps Toward a Positive Self-Image

1. Integrity is life's greatest asset.
Let's start today with the fundamental key to your progress and to life itself. *That key is integrity.* Integrity begins and flourishes when you are honest with yourself; then you can be honest with all others. Honesty with oneself is the first and foremost virtue. Without it, progressive advancement is impossible. Growth begins with honesty. It causes this newly-discovered self to glow with understanding and brightens your outlook on life.
(a)Being yourself is your highest privilege.
Each and every one of us has an equal opportunity to be true to ourselves, to discover who we are—and this opportunity is tremendous! And we are the only ones who can travel within to explore all of the "hidden treasures" that have been given to us as individual creations. Use your imagination: have you ever dreamed of exploring a hidden cavern and finding treasures in it? Your mind is like an unexplored cavern which contains "treasures" even beyond our wildest comprehensions. Will *you* take the time to search for them? Because if you do, what you find will surprise and delight you! Great things have a way of coming into our lives when we accept the attitude of self-honesty. And only when we are honest with ourselves can we be truly honest with others.
(b)   Another great quality is your individuality.
There is not even one other person who is like you, even if you are an identical twin. You were born with the capacity for determining your own place in life. You know you do not desire to follow the majority if they are wrong. You were born to be you. So be yourself! Your individuality

72

Step V – Self-Image

is your road to success. Look inside and evaluate yourself. While you are alone and your surroundings are serene, you can be honest and sincere. But there is no need to wear a "mask" when you are around others. Don't be a hypocrite. Don't give a false impression; continue to be conscious of the fact that there is nothing that will assure your personal success more than your own integrity, enthusiasm, and self-confidence. Self-confidence in your individuality can be your greatest motivator. Develop it and put it to purposeful action.

2. Take advantage of every available self-help avenue.
   The habit of overlooking self-help is a very destructive barrier to a good self-image. Learn from the mistakes of others, but do not use them as excuses for your lack of self-improvement. Too many of us are experts at detecting the faults of others, but too blind to see them in ourselves. If you dislike something in another person, remember not to commit that same fault in yourself. By being honest with yourself, you will become the person you were born to be. Your purpose for life must never be limited by a comparison with someone else. The only real competition in life is with yourself and your own potential.

In Athens, Greece, an old man in his seventies walked through the streets, gathering every child he could around him. He would sit and speak to them. As he did, the children would reach out and touch his robes. He wandered through the streets of other ancient cities teaching children. Soon he became known in the minds of the youth as a leader. The adults, however, resented and were disturbed by him. They decided to destroy him by giving him hemlock, a deadly poison which kills by slowly moving up the body, inch by inch, until it reaches the heart. They had guards surround the old man, invented charges against him, and condemned him to death.

The children gathered around and cried, "This is unkind! The old man loved us, taught us honest, personal regard, and helped

The Living Dreamer

us develop our self-image!" All to no avail. The old man was given the hemlock.

As he lay dying, the old man told the children to keep trying to understand themselves, to have self-confidence, and to carry on the thoughts and projections he had laid down for them. A small boy in the group, with tears on his face, was determined to carry on these great truths. He left the country, traveling the world, to find himself and to understand what life was all about. He came back to his homeland years later and wrote of his experiences. In essence, he laid the basic philosophy for that day and for all succeeding generations.

That old man was Socrates, and the young boy was Plato! They have been called the greatest of all Greek philosophers in a period of history called "The Golden Ages."

Conformity robs you of creativity and uniqueness. Your life is far too precious and too short to be wasted in conformity. It will steal away any resemblance of your real self.

3. Make each day count, live it up!

Live life "to the hilt" every single day. Don't waste time daydreaming about your future accomplishments and the rich life you might acquire next year. Live your life now. When today is lived properly, tomorrow will fit into place. It is important that each day be happy and meaningful. No day should ever be boring. Make it an exciting adventure.

Resolve the past and forget it. Dream big dreams, but wake up and do something today to make them come true. Study to better yourself. Dare to think great and become great. Be sure to fill your head with proper knowledge. Happiness is being prepared daily for you. You can accept it or reject it.

Abraham Lincoln once said, "It has been my observation that people are just about as happy as they make up their minds to be." Happiness is for you. Start receiving it and giving it away. Every time you give happiness to another you magnify your own happiness many, many times. Happiness is one of those rare products which multiplies by division.

Step V - Self-Image

4. Change your self-image.

Change the picture you have of yourself inside. Create the perfect you! Believe you can be an achiever in this success adventure, and you will be on the right road.

Here is another great insight for your Success Step: it is belief, not benefit, that will motivate you from one astronomical achievement to another, and then to another. Keep these basic evaluations in mind:

(a) Are you working for beliefs or benefits? Benefits can disappear, but benefits can only satisfy your physical appetites and must remain outside your true inheritance. Beliefs bring satisfaction to the deepest longings of the heart and become the star to guide your destiny. Beliefs are your true inheritances and they remain with you throughout eternity.

(b) Your beliefs will sustain you through all criticism by enabling you to have confidence in yourself. You can remain firm in your convictions when you know they are on the solid ground of your own research. You can overcome any criticism and move beyond the crowd in accomplishment.

(c) Belief will enable you to use your capabilities and abilities to their fullest possibilities, keeping you constantly dissatisfied with mediocrity.

(d) Belief is the opportunity to enable a power greater than yourself to operate within you, bringing you to levels which you could not achieve alone.

(e) If your belief brings you a discontentment about who you are, try to inspire yourself to reach the stars by a phrase used by *the living dreamer,* "What will you be ten years from now? Start being today what you desire and want to be ten years from now." It works. It will work for you.

5. Make the best use of your will.

(a) Will power is the incentive that gives us the strength to go on when others have stopped. When the will is used in the right way, it enables us to put our productive thinking into action.

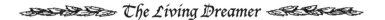

The Living Dreamer

Charles Atlas was a ninety-seven pound weakling. He became dissatisfied with his physique when his female friends were attracted to larger, better-built boys. He exercised his will power to become the best physical specimen of his day. His course inspired thousands to have healthy bodies and enabled him to taste the "fruits of success."

Another example of strong belief can be seen in a Russian family who lived on the edge of a lake near the border. They made a decision to seek their freedom. As they crossed the lake, they suddenly faced a guard's gun. He told them to walk back across the lake, for he had orders to shoot them down if they tried to cross the border. They turned around and went back across the lake where they took a family vote. The child's vote counted the same as the adult's. They voted individually as to whether they valued their freedom more than their lives. After the vote was taken, it was decided: "We either go through, or die here on the border." They went back and stood in front of the guard and said, "Either shoot us down or let us pass. We will die free."

The guard raised the gun but could not pull the trigger. Their courage paralyzed him. They are now in the "Land of the Free" because they dared to live their dream—greater than death itself!

(b) Will power serves as a magnet to draw resources from the "Infinite Intelligence." Henry Ward Beecher spoke of someone giving him a dish of sand containing particles of iron. He said he might go through the sand with his inexperienced and clumsy fingers without detecting the iron, but if he were given a magnet to sweep over the contents, it would draw the invisible particles out by the power of attraction. The will has this same kind of power to attract qualities to help us transform and accelerate ourselves. So it is very important to cultivate the will power by establishing who you want to become and what you want to accomplish.

Step V - Self-Image

(c) Eliminate the negative, nonproductiveness in your life and supplement it with positive productiveness. How well advised are the words of the old song, "Eliminate the Nonproductive and Accentuate the Productive." This song has been around for a long time, but few have taken the time to listen to its wisdom and apply it.

(d) Make decisions and act on them. An indecisive mind is the major deterrent to action. This can be seen in the following ways:
- Not admitting a problem. Hiding your head in the sand like an ostrich and pretending there is no problem is no way to overcome it!
- Running away from, and refusing to face your problems.
- Waiting for someone else to solve your problem.
- Always blaming someone else for your problems.
- Criticizing other people constantly.
- Decision and action are the result of:
- Making sure what it is you want.
- Realizing, to a large degree, its true value.
- Believing you can do it.
- Taking one step at a time.
- Putting yourself on the spot by making your intentions known.
- Beginning a pattern of achievement; creating a "Road of Success."
- Paying the price.

6. Concentration, or single-point focusing, has a way of bringing astonishing results home. It draws courage, energy, and enthusiasm for every task. (Discussed in Step II, Goals.)

Thomas A. Edison observed: "If we did all the things we are capable of doing, we would literally astound ourselves."

Ralph Waldo Emerson said: "A good intention clothes itself with sudden power."

7. Feed productive/constructive thoughts into your mind.

There is one part of you over which you can have complete control—your mind. You will be reminded many times and in many ways throughout this book that whatever the human mind can conceive and believe can be achieved. The best training of your inner mind is to "feed" it with great achievements.

The greatest individuals, of past and present history, are those who have the foresight and discipline to make a practical use of the subconscious mind.

Those believing in the power and proper exercise of the inner mind have brought reality to their aspirations. The failure to believe has brought havoc to men and women's self-image and potential. The plateaus of the past are strewn with the wreckage of fallen stars, the "could-have-beens"—while the galaxies of fulfillment are beautifully arrayed with the orbital achievements of those doers and accomplishers who believed and produced. As a great French philosopher learned: "The mind will not take the trouble to work for those who do not believe in it."

The inner mind is either/or; it is either magnificently clothed in a system of worthwhile objectives and accomplishments; or it is like a cluttered "Society's Ignore Closet," portraying the lack of a system, and not really knowing what is wrong.

We can make the subconscious carry out our orders. A simple illustration can be seen on a piece of paper. Take it, fold it; then fold it again, and again on the same fold. The impression made at the point of the fold soon weakens the fiber of the paper. It can then be easily torn at this point. The same is true of continuous commands and directions to the subconscious mind. With every repeated order come deep and lasting impressions.

Here is a very important phrase to remember—and use:
"Each time a negative thought attempts to enter my mind, some thought I don't want, I will immediately become aware of it and will dissolve it with a positive, productive, thought phrase: 'A thought just passed through me, but I will not attach a name to it…' I am programming in error, reprogram to present or perfect environment. My self-confidence is mounting as day by day I gain mastery over self. I am thankful for the great powers of mental concentration/single-point focusing. I can hold my thoughts on a single idea until I elect to discharge it from my mind. I master my being and can fully relax at will."

Step V – Self-Image

Your self-image will determine
the progress and meaning
of your Steps to Success.

Now is the accepted time—
time for the decision
Reject the "old" self-image and
Create the New Self!

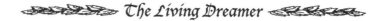 The Living Dreamer

Change Yourself and Live Your Dreams

Change brings all the pain we feel in life.
Change brings on all the joy we experience.
Change is the word we use in the hope things
will get better.
Change is the word we fear at the thought things
will turn for the worse.
Change is the promise of total understanding of
all things and unity—love.
Change is the decay to, "Don't like it as near as I should
like it."
And change is the hope that what labels you as an outcast today,
will make you acceptable tomorrow.
Change is, "Oh Boy, will I ever get through
this thing."
It is also, "I hope it never ends."
Change is your opportunity for a better way of life.

Change your self-image
And take a new lease on life!

The Coming of The Dreamer

I will never forget that morning and the incredible realization that came to me in that one single moment of recognition. It was as if my entire life had been spent passing time and waiting for this one day to arrive...

It was just before dawn, and the sky was still faintly sprinkled with starlight. The birds had not yet begun their enthusiastic welcome to the morning sun. This was my favorite time of day, and I had often walked quietly through the courtyard to contemplate and collect my thoughts. I remember how the gentle breeze brushed against my skin, and how everything seemed so quiet and still. So serene. Only, on this morning a song had come to my lips. It was one that I had not heard before. My ears listened to it for the first time as I let the beautiful sounds flow effortlessly from somewhere within. This was the first time that I had heard my own singing voice. And when the song had ceased, almost as if in answer, birdsong sprung from the surrounding trees in such magnitude, that I knew they were responding to what they had just heard.

In that one single moment IT hit me. I caught my breath, and sat down on the dewy morning grass. The feelings were too intense. Was this yet another step in the greater comprehension of the unknown within? Had I finally reached an understanding that surpassed the "ordinary" person? Or was this just my overactive imagination working overtime? No! I had arrived at an even greater realization of who I am and, even more importantly, of Why I am! And if what I was feeling and now recognizing within my mind was the truth, then time would give me the answers and which path I was "destined" to take. Right now, there was no doubt that what I was feeling was as close to knowing my true and higher self, as I had ever witnessed or even imagined possible.

The cool morning air caressed my face, and the soft wetness of the fresh-cut lawn had penetrated to my skin. I shivered, but I wasn't cold. I was feeling so elated!

The Living Dreamer

I noticed that the birdsong had stopped, almost as if they were waiting in unison for a response. I did not hesitate and offered my own spontaneous, morning song to the winged creatures as they silently listened—and then joined in. The morning air filled with the most radiant expressions of joy for living that I will ever know.

Almost as if on cue, a brilliant, luminous, golden light burst from the horizon, and I was overwhelmed by a sense of belonging. It was as if I was coming home. It was an emotion I had never felt before. It was a sense of being connected—to all things. And a feeling of uniqueness and meaning as an individual creation.

I will be able to relive that morning—every moment, every sight and sound—as if I were sent back in time and living it all over again. That's when I knew who I was. I came to know a feeling that seemed to surpass and rise above earthly expressions. It was a sense of knowing that there is so much more than what "meets the eye." It was scraping away all of the debris that had collected upon a life that had been pushed and shoved in all the wrong directions, or even no direction at all; maybe just pushed aside.

All of us are on our own private journeys, through time and space. The destination? Whoever it is we wish to become. But if we do not venture into the unknown with our minds, we will not come to know and understand who we are and why we are here. Sometimes it may be by "accident," or it may be by planning and investigating all of the resources that are available within our reach.

Whatever it takes to find the person you were meant to be, do it! The only thing any of us have to lose is the life that we have not yet lived. And it could be the most incredible journey! You, too, could be living that sought-after life, instead of being the one who just reads about it!

Take the time, and venture into the unknown. Get to know the inner you, because this is the real you. You will experience a feeling that is well worth knowing, and it gives you a sense of being more than human. And if I had to describe it in one word, when I came to know and understand that wonderful "being" within, the one word that comes to mind, is...a dreamer. But then, didn't you already somehow know that? Because that is who is calling you right now...

Step VI
Self-Discipline

Self-discipline is an important requirement for individual success and yields a most satisfactory result. Self-discipline has a great effect on your health and happiness. Without it, nothing falls into place or stays that way.

There are some distinctive assets that you acquire while practicing self-discipline:
- Your faith in yourself grows as you begin to reap inner resources in your life.
- Your personality blossoms. People who never looked your way will begin to seek you out.
- Your self-confidence increases daily.
- The world looks different.
- Tasks become easier as you become conditioned to their demands.
- Your hopes and ambitions gain strength and fulfillment.
- Your imagination becomes more alert.
- Your enthusiasm has deeper roots and greater influence.
- Your situations are worked out and do not become problems.
- What appeared to be difficult is much easier to overcome.
- Your overall health improves.
- Your initiative becomes keener and you take on new enterprises with greater desire.
- Your vision is greatly enlarged.

By developing self-discipline, you are taking "possession" of your mind. You are taking possession of it with such strength that the emotions, the instincts, and the body are brought under your control.

The Living Dreamer

Therefore, self-discipline begins with your thoughts. People who do not control their thoughts are unable to control their actions.

It is through the power of self-discipline that you can balance the emotions of the heart with the reasoning of the mind. This is done by the right use of will power. In the creation of man and woman, the "Universal Infinite Intelligence" gave each of them a will of their own.

We can use this will power to destroy our lives, or build them. When used properly, it can help us develop a love for ourselves in the highest sense. This self-love is the first step in learning to "love thy neighbor." People who love themselves more than food will never be gluttons; who love themselves more than personal gain will never become greedy; who loves themselves more than drugs will never become addicts.

Everyone has an ego with which they can balance their natural urges with the society-accepted "norms" of our culture. The ego, acting through the will, is like a "coach" guiding the body and mind through self-discipline. When the ego is not trained and made strong, the body and the mind take their own course, and are very susceptible to outside events.

There is an old song, "Doing What Comes Naturally," which quite possibly explains how the greatest segment of our population is motivated—much to their jeopardy.

Animals that cannot adapt to the environment they are in will soon die. People who adapt themselves to cynical, destructive attitudes and to the behavior of the cynics and disillusioned, soon "die" to all that is of the best and beautiful. An example: people who "save face," or to always defend themselves, and always say they're right while everyone else is wrong, will be kept forever out of touch with reality.

Another great advantage of self-discipline is its power and protection. People controlling themselves through self-discipline can never be controlled by others. Self-discipline is the only means by which one can focus the mind upon the objective of a worthwhile purpose. Love then moves the will to the heights of achievement and satisfaction.

Self-discipline is indispensable in all types of leadership. The Bible speaks of people being unable to follow when the trumpet gives an uncertain sound. This is another way of declaring an old truth that leaders must exercise the greatest of care and the greatest self-discipline to inspire others to a higher and better way.

Step VI – Self-Discipline

Self-discipline is essential for becoming a success. You are the only one capable of acquiring self-discipline, *for it must come from the inner person.*

First, you must believe you can succeed, and with your self-discipline intact, go about doing exactly that.

For many years it was generally accepted that it was impossible to run a mile in four minutes. A lanky, frail-looking English physician named Roger Bannister, disproved that fact when he ran the mile in four minutes in 1954. Why had no one ever run the mile that fast before? Bannister feels it was because people did not believe that it could be done.

In 1886, a man ran the mile in $4:12:^3/_4$ minutes, a world record for 37 years. In 1923, a winning run of $4:10:^3/_4$ minutes was recorded. It wasn't until 1954 that this record was topped by Bannister. Since then, many other runners have run the mile in less than four minutes! Bannister attributes this change as being psychological rather than improved styles of running. Once the four-minute mile had been run, the idea was accepted—*it could be done!* This is one example of how self-discipline paid off through consistent conditioning and effort.

Roll with the punches. This is another way of saying let go, and don't let the "in" pressures "out" pressure you.

The following true story illustrates the importance of calm, emotional control in doing a vital job. The aircraft carrier, Essex, was entering Pearl Harbor loaded with planes and gear from San Francisco and carrying five thousand Marines. The officers and men in Pearl Harbor were eager to see the first of the replacement ships, and her arrival was a significant event of the war.

As the ship entered the channel, a fire broke out on the hangar deck. Simultaneously, a merchant ship was sighted coming out. The channel at Pearl Harbor was not wide enough for two ships under normal conditions, and the situation was critical.

Word of the fire was passed to the bridge and the officer of the deck called to the captain, "Fire on the hangar deck!" Because of the proximity of fuel and ammunition storage, a fire on the deck was a

The Living Dreamer

serious matter. The captain was closely watching the approaching ship and did not appear to have heard, so the officer of the deck repeated his report, more loudly.

Without turning his head, the captain, who was noted for his imperturbability, said quietly, "Put it out."

The two ships passed safely, and the fire was put out with little damage.

Get busy achieving your desired objectives, and soon you'll forget you thought that they couldn't be done. Become aware of the productive elements of hope. Establish confidence in your capacity to find a way in every circumstance.

Young Ben Franklin was certain he was a good writer, and wanted to prove it. His brother, James, who owned the newspaper where he had apprenticed, had no faith in Ben's literary talents, and refused to print his work.

Knowing his brother was prejudiced towards him, and thought of him only as a pesky, young scamp, Ben tried to think of a way to get James to publish his work without him knowing it. Finally, he decided to sign all of his work as "Poor Richard," and slip it under the door of the printing shop each night after his brother had left.

As Ben had expected, his brother was delighted with Poor Richard's work and was happy to print it. His column became popular with the readers, and Ben went on in a few years to publish his own journal called "Poor Richard's Almanac."

Take some time out right now and ask yourself some very important questions:
* What are you going to do with these suggestions?
* Are you a leader or a follower?
* Have you applied anything that you have learned so far?
* Do you grasp the initiative, or do you wait to be told what to do?

When you desire to be a success, you must develop self-discipline. You have to expend the effort and do the work before

Step VI – Self-Discipline

you receive the compensation. For you to be successful you must feel you deserve success. You cannot lie to yourself. You have an amazing ability to fool others, but you will never fool yourself. So you must become a success in your own mind first, and *then* you will be able to reap the benefits.

Don't fail as some people you may know who are "know-it-alls." Just remember, it is what you learn, after you think you know it all, that is important.

Self-discipline will greatly enhance your self-improvement. It will channel you into good habits of learning and accomplishing something new each day.

When the day is over you should be able to look back and say to yourself, "Even though a full day of my life is gone, the price I have paid was not wasted. I have contributed and received a full measure in return."

Be proud of your accomplishments. Train and condition yourself to reach higher each day. Take a good and honest inventory. Are you growing?

Look forward to life with new meaning and new interests, knowing that you are participating in the overall growth of humanity. And it is because you have disciplined yourself to assure your personal growth.

You must become a self-starter!

How? Do it now! Don't procrastinate. Be willing to wind your own motor. Motivate yourself to action. The reason your boss earns more than you is because he or she is paid to motivate you and others to get the job done.

A self-starter attracts leadership. You will climb your stairway to success at a rapid pace when you decide to motivate yourself, take the initiative, and be a leader.

Since you spend a large part of your time listening to yourself, and since we have learned that you can control your mind—why not start right now telling yourself you are a winner? This will provide the incentive for the necessary action to achieve great things *and* you will deserve them.

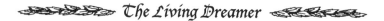 The Living Dreamer

Tell yourself you are great, believe it, and great you will become.

Never lose sight of the vital importance of a self-disciplined mind. *Focus your thoughts, and your actions will focus themselves.* You can become whoever it is you desire, regardless of what you have been or what you are at this moment. Because you make the decisions, and you are more than willing to do something about it.

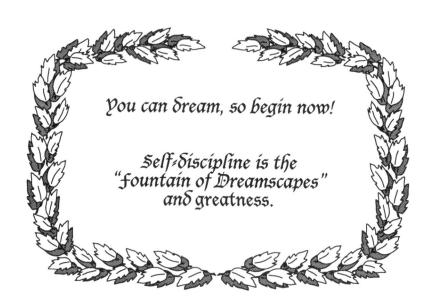

You can dream, so begin now!

Self-discipline is the "Fountain of Dreamscapes" and greatness.

Step VII
Relationships With People

One of the reasons you are participating in this success journey is because of a desire to improve your day-to-day relationships with all people. You want to be liked. The joy of being accepted and appreciated by others is an important skill that can (and must!) be mastered.

The famed philosopher and dean of St. Paul's Cathedral in London, John Donne, wrote that no man or woman is an island entire of itself. Each is "a piece of the continent, a part of the main...any (man/woman's) death diminishes me, because I am involved in Mankind; and therefore never send to know for whom the bell tolls; it tolls for you."

We were not meant to stand alone, nor to live and die unto ourselves. Every man and every woman is "involved in Mankind." The world is made up of people needing other people. Our greatest happiness comes from our relationship with our Creator and with our fellow individuals.

Consider the following seven ways to improve your relationships with others:

1. Seek to make yourself likable by your love and a genuine concern for others. Make the most of your personality and appearance. Always wear your best smile; no one cares for a "sourpuss."
2. It is very important to remember people's names. A person's name, to them, is the sweetest and most important sound, in any language. More friends can be made in two months by showing genuine interest in people than can be made in two years by trying to make them interested in you. Your interest is shown when you remember someone's name; be it a man, a woman or a child.

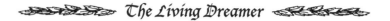

3. Openly express appreciation for what others do. The psychologist William James stated: "The deepest principle in human nature is the craving to be appreciated." It is best to forget what you have done for others but *always remember what others have done for you.* Be hearty in your appreciation and lavish in your praise. Notice even the slightest improvement and comment on it. This will also inspire others to keep on improving. Praising people opens the door for helping them at a later time to overcome their faults. Seek to find the best in others, and you will be amazed at how much you will discover. The most important trait you can have is the ability to see the best in them.
4. Listen intently to other people's words. Most of the people you meet are hungry and thirsty for understanding and appreciation. When you give them this, you will be greatly loved and admired.
5. Let the interests of the other people be the topic of conversation. This will enable them to express themselves and help you to know and understand them better. Never assume a bored attitude or permit an "I knew it" expression to flicker across your face. When you interrupt others, you are implying that what they are saying is not worthy of your attention or your time. Talk to them about subjects that interest them, and they will become your friends.
6. Make the other people feel important. One of the best means of establishing good relationships with others is to give consideration to their opinions. You are never more important to another person than when you open for them an opportunity to feel important.
7. Beware of criticism and nonproductiveness in your conversation and bearing. As Benjamin Franklin wisely advised: "Any fool can criticize, condemn and complain—and most fools do." Who has ever seen a statue erected to a critic? There is always a reason for a person acting as they do. Given enough opportunities, they will give you the key to their personality and attitudes.

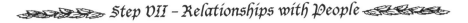# Step VII - Relationships with People

Some tried and proven suggestions for putting these rules into practice are:

1. Learn to be courteous and helpful in ways that are meaningful to others.

    One of the greatest examples of courtesy in history has survived for 400 years. Many people don't remember Sir Walter Raleigh for his exploration of the state of Virginia and his other great accomplishments, but his manners and courtesy will always be well remembered.

    Raleigh was out walking in the palace gardens one day with Queen Elizabeth. It had been raining, and on the path before them was a puddle of water. Rather than allow Queen Elizabeth to walk through the puddle, Raleigh took off his new velvet cloak and laid it in the water for the Queen to walk on.

    This is only one example of the many courtesies known by Sir Walter Raleigh. Because of them, the Queen was so impressed with him that she sponsored and paid for his many explorations. He rapidly rose to a high place in the court.

    The word courtesy comes from court, meaning "the politeness that is practiced in the refinement of a court of royalty."

"The small courtesies sweeten life. The great courtesies ennoble it." Since we are all emotional beings and respond in kind to the emotions of others, a courteous attitude towards someone gives us the same response from them. Our personality is determined to a great extent by the way we treat other people.

Louisa May Alcott, the famous 19th century author of Little Women *and other books beloved by all, learned a very important lesson in courtesy at an early age.*

At her fourteenth birthday party, she wore a crown of flowers and stood on a table to give the other children cakes as they passed by her. She writes of the incident in her diary.

"By some oversight the cakes fell short, and I saw that if I gave the last one I should have none. As I was queen of the party, I felt I ought to have it. I held on to it tightly till my dear mother *said, "It is always better to give away than to keep the nice things, so I know my 'Louey' will not let her little friend go without."*

The friend got the cake, and Louisa received her first lesson in the sweetness of courtesy and consideration to others; a lesson that was to serve her well all her life.

William Pitt, Lord Chathem, once remarked, "Now as to politeness, I would rather venture to call it benevolence in trifles." Charles Dickens, well known for his courtesy to others, said, "Once a gentleman, always a gentleman." The real mark of a gentleman is how he treats others who can benefit him in no particular way. Be courteous to other people, no matter how unimportant they might be, and courtesy will be returned, over and over.

2. Treat others as you would like to be treated.

All the major religions of the world express, in some way, the same admonition: "Do unto others as you want them to do unto you." This is the most important point to remember in your relationships with people.

The gigantic empire of J.C. Penney was based on this same foundation. When he was a young boy, his father—a poor farmer and part-time preacher—taught him that consideration, honesty and fairness to others was more important than monetary rewards. It was a lesson he never forgot. The first store Penney opened was called "The Golden Rule Store." Through years of struggle with ill health and financial hardships, Mr. Penney survived on this same "Golden Rule" principle. He was always trying to bring to his customers the best merchandise for the least money. His rise to the position of a successful tycoon was patterned on the belief of fairness and consideration to others.

In Mr. Penney's office on the 45th floor of a skyscraper named after him, a wall is hung with many honors accumulated throughout his long life. In the center of this wall hangs the motto on which he built his great fortune: "Do unto others as you would have them do unto you."

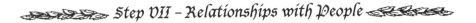

Step VII - Relationships with People

If you don't approve of the way someone acts, take the time to look behind his or her actions and see what he or she is really like. You will notice that as you help someone to be his or her true self, you not only have the satisfaction of knowing you have had a part in the success, but your own self-esteem will get a boost in the awareness that you have given your best to another. You have treated them the way you would want them to treat you.

When you desire to be a power among individuals, meet them and treat them with enthusiasm. People will like you better for it and you will escape the dull routine of a mechanical existence. You will make headway wherever you are. Put your heart and soul into bettering your relationships with others, and they will believe and trust in you.

3. Listen to what people are trying to express. Try to help them find their true direction.

Average people are wrapped up in their own selves. They are so intent in listening to themselves, they never listen to anyone else. Be different—lend an ear to your fellow friend.

General George Marshall stated it this way:
"Listen to the other person's story.
Listen to the other person's full story.
Listen to the other person's full story first!"

A newspaper editor in a small town often worked until late at night in his office. One night about midnight, there was a knock on his door. "Come in," he called. The door opened and there was the forlorn figure of a neighbor; a man whose son had recently drowned while out canoeing with his parents. The canoe had overturned; the man and his wife were saved, but the child did not survive.

Since that tragedy, the father had been extremely depressed. On this night, he had apparently been out walking the street and been drawn by the light in the newspaper office.

He came in and sat down, slumping forward in dejection and silence. Instead of making conversation, the editor went on with his work. After a few minutes the neighbor said, "I'm ready to talk."

The Living Dreamer

He poured out his heart for more than an hour. He told again the details of that fateful night, and wondered out loud if he could have done anything more to save his son. Finally, he talked himself out. He asked if he could come and talk again, and then he left.

The editor had done nothing but listen attentively, with sympathy and a loving heart. He was esteemed by everyone in his town because of his ability to listen. People came to talk their problems over with him and in so doing, found their own solutions. What a wonderful asset he was to the community!

The North American continent would not have been discovered by Europeans in 1492 if Queen Isabella of Spain had not taken the time to listen to Christopher Columbus. Because this great woman was interested in and willing to listen to the hopes and dreams of an itinerant merchant sailor from Italy, her wealth was increased many times over.

There are many excellent books we can read to enlighten and encourage our lives. One of which is Og Mandino's *The Greatest Salesman in the World*. It contains scrolls which we might well claim as our own. These are to be used wisely, for they will take us farther than we could ever imagine on our own. Display them where they can be seen at all times, for they will last a lifetime.

4. Be conscious of the needs of others and give your best to meet those needs.

Napoleon Bonaparte said, "I love power. Yes, I love it, but after the manner of an artist, as a fiddler in order to conjure from it—tones, chords, harmony."

Therefore, the real key is to decide on what you want to do with your success, and the reasoning behind your decision. If you can use it for the benefit of others, then there is a worthy reason for seeking it.

And you will find that on so many occasions, when you are fulfilling the needs of others, your own needs will also be met.

Step VII – Relationships with People

5. Be willing to go the "extra mile."

Everyone who becomes involved with the principles of *The Living Dreamer* will go the extra mile out of an inborn desire to help others; to live life to the extent it was meant, and to produce at the highest levels possible. There is also a mutual feeling of independent pride as the individual becomes an achiever and feels like he ro she is part of a winning team.

Anne Sullivan is one of the finest illustrations of a person who was willing to go the extra mile.

Miss Sullivan was a teacher at the Perkins Institute for the Blind, and was given the job of teaching eight-year-old Helen Keller to talk. However, it appeared to be an overwhelming task. The child had suffered a severe illness at the age of two years and was not only blind, but also deaf. Little Helen was lost in a strange world and terrified by everything she couldn't see or hear. She was like a wild animal, and it seemed an impossible task to even reach her.

Miss Sullivan did reach her, but only because she went the extra mile. Instead of trying merely to teach the child, she put her entire soul, her entire life into giving love and understanding and help to that frightened, lonely child. She gave of herself over and above what anyone could have asked from her.

The whole world knows the story of her success. Not only did Helen Keller learn to communicate with others, she graduated with honors from Radcliffe College, gained renown as an author, and became one of the world's most inspirational public figures.

Without Anne Sullivan's willingness—even more than that, her eagerness—to go the extra mile, Helen Keller might well have remained lost in a world of dark silence, and the earth would have been a poorer place indeed for not having known this well-loved woman.

6. Let love motivate your attitude and every action.

Hate is an attitude no one can afford. Just a few minutes of hate burns up as much energy as hard work does in eight hours.

The Living Dreamer

And love is the only power strong enough to move the will of humankind to its highest self.

Kahlil Gibran wrote in his beloved book *Secrets of the Heart:* "Love is the house of true fortune, and the origin of pleasure, and the beginning of peace and tranquility."

One business man carries a card which reads: "The way to happiness: Keep your heart free from hate, your mind from worry. Live simply, expect little, give much. Fill your life with love. Scatter sunshine. Forget self. Think of others. Do as you would be done by."

This is a wonderful formula for letting love motivate your attitudes and acts. When put into action, it enables you to remain poised and confident in any situation. Try it for a week; you'll be surprised how it changes your life!

7. Live above petty criticism.

Jane Adams, well known founder of the Hull House in Chicago, grew up in a well-off family. While she was a young child, her father brought her to one of the mills he owned in a slum district. Jane was horrified at the conditions in the area that the people were forced to live under. She decided at that time, that when she grew up, she would do something to help them.

She never forgot this determined dream of hers. When she was older, she bought a great house in the slum district of Chicago and named it Hull Settlement House. Her friends were horrified. They begged her not to continue with her plans, and to live a "normal" life instead, one that befitted a young lady of her status. When Jane refused, she was severely criticized and ridiculed as a "do-gooder."

Miss Adams ignored the unfavorable talk however, and continued with her work. Her concern for others was rewarded many times by the love that was returned. Her name has gone down in history as one of the great humanitarians of the past century.

And Clara Barton, who founded the American Red Cross, was once reminded by a friend of some rather violent criticism

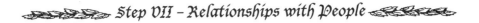

Step VII – Relationships with People

that had been leveled at her a few years before. Miss Barton seemed not to recall it.

"Don't you remember it?" asked her friend.

"No," she replied, "I distinctly remember forgetting it!"

8. Desire the best for those who seem to take advantage of you.

A merchant who owned a small independent clothes shop in a run-down neighborhood of a large city was almost bankrupt. He had always had his customers charge their merchandise. But at this time there was a recession, and the people were not paying their bills. His own debts had been mounting up; soon he would be forced to close the store.

One day, he was talking his problem over with his minister, and the minister suggested, "Why don't you make an effort to find out the needs and problems of your customers. Get interested in them. When you send out each bill, write a personal note in it telling them you wish them well. As you mail out each bill, take time to say a short prayer for that person; not that your bill will be paid, but that he can overcome his problems and that his needs will be met."

The owner was skeptical, but out of desperation he decided to try it. The response was a tremendous surprise! Of the 127 people who owed him money, over half paid part of their bill and some paid all of it. His business began picking up as the rest of his customers also responded.

Soon he was back on his feet and business was better than it had ever been before.

9. Recognize the importance of every individual you meet.

Sometimes the people you meet casually need your understanding and love more than your friends. Everybody is somebody in the "Creator's Sight." The stronger this attitude is, the greater the assistance will be that you bring to others, and the larger the delight will be in your life.

There is a very beloved lady who takes the time to get very acquainted with every person she meets, and treats each as the

The Living Dreamer

most important person in her world. She is a woman of genuine sincerity who is truly interested in her fellow person—whether president of a bank, shop clerk, or a homeless person asking for a handout.

One day she stopped at a street corner where a man in a wheelchair was selling little household gadgets he had made. She talked with him for a while and bought one of his gadgets.

Each time she passed that particular corner after this, no matter how hurried she was, she stopped to chat with the "Gadget Man." It was after she had gotten to know him fairly well and had shown how interested she was in him, that he trusted her enough to tell his story.

He was an unhappy, embittered man who felt rejected by the world. Born and raised in bleak poverty, he had been cut down as a young man by a tragic accident which left him paralyzed in both legs. Doctors had told him an operation could restore the use of his legs. However, the operation was an expensive one, and would involve months of convalescence and rehabilitation.

He had no money and there was no one in his life who cared. His parents and all of his close relatives were dead. Hope for a normal life was gone and he was a miserable, despondent man.

The lady was extremely touched by his story and determined to do something to help him.

Because of her great interest in people, she had made friends in all walks of life, including people of great influence. She visited all of them and asked for donations. She persuaded the local newspaper to publish the story. Contributions were soon pouring in. Doctors volunteered their services.

Within six weeks, the man was able to have the necessary operation. There was money left over to provide for his recovery period. He took this opportunity to study and further his education.

His kind and loving friend visited him often, and cards and letters of encouragement continued to pour in. He was rapidly finding that most people were basically good; that more people cared than he had ever imagined.

~~~~ Step VII – Relationships with People ~~~~

This happened a few years ago. The man is now working in the bookkeeping department of a small business firm. He has found self-respect, hope and encouragement. Today, he is a truly happy man with his own bookkeeping accounting firm. And it's all because of a wonderful lady who considered him important.

10. Have a strong belief that there is a way to achieve the best results.

A major key to success is to give it all you've got. A famous athletic coach once said that the trouble with most people, athletes as well as non-athletes, is that they always hold something in reserve.

A trapeze artist was instructing students in how to perform on the trapeze bar. After giving a full explanation in this skill, he told them to demonstrate their ability. One student, looking up at the perch on which he was to perform, was suddenly filled with fear. He froze completely and gasped, "I can't do it!"

The instructor put his arm around the boy's shoulder and said, "Son, you can do it and I'll tell you how. Throw your heart over the bar and your body will follow."

Psychologists, through studies, have learned that people spend most of their time thinking about themselves. And yet, life's real growth comes when we think of others and how to relate to them. Good human relations is the result of a heartfelt concern for others. This concern expresses itself in a persuasive personality tempered with grace and humility, free of irritation and confusion.

A "Capsule Course" in Human Relations:

5 most important words:	I am proud of you.
4 most important words:	What is your opinion?
3 most important words:	If you please.
2 most important words:	Thank you.
The least important word:	I

The Living Dreamer

Simmons has said, "A quick and sound judgment; a good common sense; kind feelings; and instinctive perception of character; in these are the elements of what is called tact, which has so much to do with acceptability and success in life."

Steed has said, "I've known some men possessed of good qualities which were very serviceable to others, and useless to themselves—like a sundial in front of a house to inform others, but not the owner within."

Tact is a universal language—mother tongue to some, foreign to others. Tactfulness will open many doors for outstanding achievement. Practice it and you will be a happier person.

Step VII – Relationships with People

"It's the hand we clasp with an honest grasp
that gives us a hearty thrill.
It's the good we pour into others' lives
that comes back our own to fill.
It's the dregs we drain from another's cup
that makes our own seem sweet;
and the hours we give to another's need
that makes our life complete.

It's the burdens we help another bear
that makes our own seem light.
It's the danger seen for another's feet
that shows us the path to right.
It's the good we do each passing day
with a heart sincere and true,
in giving the world your very best
its best will return to you."

— Author Unknown

Give—Listen—Understand!
Go the Extra Mile!

Adventure III
Merlin and King Arthur

"What is *thinking*?" asked King Arthur.

Merlin replied, "Thinking is what made you ask me what thinking is."

"Thinking is seeing things from the perspective of the height of a hawk," Merlin remarked.

"Make me a hawk then, so that I, too, will understand," said King Arthur.

Merlin made him a hawk. He was flying high in the sky when Merlin asked, "What can you see?"

"I can see the trees and the lake all at one time," replied King Arthur.

"Can you see as far as Camelot?" asked Merlin.

"Yes," answered King Arthur.

"Can you see the outer boundary of the Kingdom?" Merlin asked.

"Yes! I can see it very clearly," King Arthur said.

"When you are down here on the ground, can you see the perimeter and the same things that you see up there—only down here, don't you see them in your imagination (or visual section) of your mind?"

"Yes," said King Arthur.

"Then, think, man, think!" said Merlin.

Perspective Aware Thinking

There can be no change in the way you react to your everyday situations unless you somehow and in some way become a perspective aware thinker. In fact, it is important for you to know that this is your language-of-the-mind and your thoughts can (and

The Living Dreamer

do!) actually control every action that your body presents to the surrounding environment.

There is a special kind of thinking that you can and must learn, for it will give you a special "power" over yourself. This special thinking is what will allow you to modify any negative, nonproductive thought or action that you do not desire, and changes it to a constructive/productive one. This is something that one dreams about most of one's life; one who seeks change from experiencing negative and nonproductive body languages, body actions, and behaviors. Now, it is yours for the keeping.

Step VIII
Possibility Thinking

You now have insight into the exciting powers that are within you, and know that you can start living a life of possibilities instead of discouragement. It is time to fully realize your new self; the one that is possible when you control and change your way of thinking.

Life is meant to be wonderful and interesting, an exciting adventure, and never a bore. This is the way it was intended to be and this is the way it can be for you. You have discovered that your life is a reflection of your thinking, just as children are reflections of their parent's actions. You must be open and willing to accept the responsibility for favorable results in your life. However, to achieve favorable results, you need to think in favorable terms.

There are many possibilities in your life which you may not have considered. Possibility thinking is going to open doors to your potential that will amaze and delight you more than anything else. For years, others have probably seen more in you than you have seen in yourself. It's time for you to grow into what is expected of you.

There is an amazing axiom about life:

When you think in nonproductive, negative terms, you can then expect negative results. When you think in productive, positive terms, then you can expect productive results. And this is precisely what is going to happen.

Humankind's greatest enemy is nonproductive and nonconstructive thinking. It can cause doubt, fear and worry. Consider some of the following statistics that come under the "heading" of worry:
- Eighteen million Americans are suffering from some form of mental illness—about one out of every ten.

The Living Dreamer

- Mental illness costs taxpayers almost three billion dollars a year.
- More people commit suicide than die from the five most common communicable diseases.
- Over 12,000 people died as a result of ulcers in 1968.
- During World War II, 330,000 Americans were killed in combat. During the same span of time, two million Americans died of heart disease. Over one million of these deaths were caused, most likely, by worry and fear. Worry is the cause of heartbreak, failure, misunderstanding and most unhappiness.
- During World War II, over two-and-a-half million Americans were rejected for induction in the Armed Forces because of mental illness—approximately one out of every six.
- Seventy percent of all patients attended by physicians could cure themselves by eliminating their inner fears and worries. Emotional stress and anxiety result in nervous indigestion, stomach ulcers, heart disturbances, insomnia and headaches.

We live in a society of "worrying people." There are those who worry so much they even worry about their worries. Montaigne, the French philosopher and writer, said, "My life has been full of terrible misfortunes, most of which never happened."

Try this formula for overcoming worry:
1. Realize that most of the things you worry about will never happen.
2. Ask yourself, "What is the worst thing that can possibly happen?"
3. Prepare to accept it with the slight possibility that you may have to.
4. Calmly proceed to improve on the worst situation, should it arise.
5. Pick out the best lessons of life for each day.
6. Practice living one day at a time.
7. Don't try to "cross a bridge" until you get there.

It has become evident that people who do not discover how to fight worry usually live an unhealthy, unpleasant life, and will probably die before they reach old age. In your climb out to mediocrity towards success, there will be some deceptive rungs on the ladder. Some of the more dangerous ones are worry, self-pity, fear, guilt, and

Step VIII - Possibility Thinking

nonproductive, negative thinking. Look forward to overcoming them. Step on them, crush them, and continue your climb.

Let's analyze these pitfalls more closely. Whether or not you profit from them will depend on how you have used the past experiences you have gone through. If you use the experiences you have had for your progress, or if you use them to further your discouragement. Circumstances surrounding us are usually brought on by our state of mind. Therefore, *choose* the optimistic state of mind. Reduce the circumstances to their proper size before acting on them. As you continue developing and polishing your attitude, you will be growing in the process, and absorbing more meaning from life.

But before any progress can be made, you have to learn to deal with a terrible enemy. It is called self-pity. It is the most destructive emotion you can have. Self-pity is an excuse and never a reason, for inaction. It can and will destroy your desire and initiative for progress. *Never feel sorry for yourself!* This contributes *absolutely nothing* to your purpose, and it steals your usefulness from being able to achieve beautiful things. Don't burn up energy feeling sorry for yourself. Use this energy to burn up the inconsistencies and hindrances to your life— especially self-pity.

Self-pity is such an alluring trap that many individuals fall into it before they realize it. It is a means of getting consoling attention and making yourself believe you have expended your best efforts. Be conscious of this trap and avoid it. A mature individual will eliminate it completely.

Some people convince themselves that they have never received enough breaks in life. These people fail to realize that their own breaks come through consistent efforts. Others feel that they have not received enough guidance and help. You will find that the biggest helping hand is at the end of your own arm!

Here is a simple formula that is very effective in overcoming any form of self-pity: Tell yourself you desire the strength and the direction to do the task and give yourself the challenge to fulfill the purpose. And make your thoughts your prayers twenty-four hours a day.

Worry is major hazard we should all avoid. This devastating and crippling attitude can consume more energy, and in a shorter time period, than both physical and mental exercises combined!

The Living Dreamer

If you must worry, then there is only one way to worry properly: Through the week compile a list, writing down everything you think you should worry about. Then on Friday afternoon at 5:00 p.m., sit back in an easy chair with your worry list—and worry. Worry about each item listed. Then worry about all of them together. If you wait until the end of the week to worry, setting aside some "worry time" to do so, you can get your work done, and you won't have time to worry.

Sounds silly, doesn't it? Worrying is silly. It is so silly that you should avoid it. Replace "worried" thoughts with pleasant thoughts. It is estimated that ninety-two percent of what we worry about either never materializes or is something that we have no control over anyway; so why waste time and energy worrying? It never solves a situation!

Past circumstances have nothing to do with future events. There is no such thing as habitual failing unless you habitually think you are going to fail. Don't "fertilize" mental blocks. When your desire to exceed is strong enough, you do not have time to worry. When the voice of worry calls, hang up the phone! Don't let worry command you—command yourself! Develop the habit of deciding for yourself what is going to be stored in your mind. Discard the belief that the power you now have is all you will ever have. This type of thinking is false and will weaken your initiative and self-confidence. You are just beginning to use your potential. Lock your mind in the gear of the productive side of life and get "turned on." Stay this way long enough, and you will never want to be in neutral or reverse again.

Begin each day with possibility thinking. Anticipate good things. As the events of the day unfold, remember to adhere to this same attitude. Carefully examine each new situation or circumstance. Picture it as it really is, not as you think it appears. Face it head on. Every adversity is the beginning of an equal or greater benefit.

Develop the philosophy that each event in our lives, good or bad, adds to our experience and prepares us for greater things. With this attitude, we can shout, "That's good!" about all situations. We'll be able to keep tuned in and turned on to the best things in life.

A right mental attitude is totally productive. A Tennessee mountain hillbilly once said, "Don't 'figger' how you can't; 'figger' how you can."

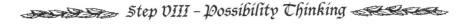

Step VIII – Possibility Thinking

Your greatest accomplishments will come from reversing nonproductive feelings. When all doors seem closed to an objective, possibility thinking will find a key.

During World War II, a man took his family on a trip to Dallas, Texas. He was told there was no place for his family to stay. Even real estate agencies failed to find a place for them. Deciding to take matters into his own hands, he rented a taxi to drive him over to the city. Soon he saw a sign advertising the sale of a large estate. He contacted the caretaker from whom he obtained the owner's name and address. Before the day was over, he had convinced the owner that the house would be more salable if someone were living in it and could show it at any hour. That night, he and his family were staying in one of the finest homes in the city at a very nominal rent. His possibility thinking refused to accept "No" as an answer and helped him overcome all obstacles.

Many never even start their climb to success, and the majority of those who do become so engrossed in discouragement, nonproductive and negative thinking, that they give up or slow down to a crawl. You deserve better than this!

Fear of failing will many times prevent you from even attempting something new. Neutralize your fears through positive action. Challenge your fears. No one really minds an honest mistake. You can gain experience from your mistakes and use them as stepping stones. You will be remembered for your successes, not your mistakes.

Everyone remembers Babe Ruth. He hit a total of 714 home runs, and is remembered today as the world's greatest slugger. What most people don't realize, and are not even concerned with, is the fact that Babe Ruth also held the world's record for the greatest number of strikeouts, a total of 1,330! He did not fear failure; his desire was to win! What he taught us is they you must get into life and start swinging! You may miss a few, but until you start swinging you will never hit any, and you'll never have a chance for a home run.

The Living Dreamer

Defeat may be a stepping stone or a stumbling block, depending upon the way you react to it. There is an old saying, "The rugged bumps on the mountain are what you climb on." This is an excellent saying to focus on whenever you are in doubt of how to react to a situation.

Do you have guilt feelings? Guilt feelings can be constructive as you relieve them through a feeling of indebtedness that results in good acts. Many of the world's greatest philanthropists were only trying to make up for some unsatisfactory event they could not erase from their lives. When you have done something wrong, don't punish yourself or become entrapped in thinking this is going to be your trend. Most of all, don't provide excuses for your mistakes. Become more aware of your actions. Channel your thinking. Motivate yourself to action—to constructive action.

The amazing result of nonproductive and negative thinking is—if you think in negative terms you will get negative results. This being true, why think in nonproductive ways? That is, unless you *want* to fail.

Your resistance to negativism will act as a strengthening force. Be optimistic and take the productive side; you will be taking the side that produces results. Use your greatest gift in life—don't shortchange yourself because it was given free. Put your mind to work on the productive and positive side.

Nonproductive, negative thinking can destroy the finest potential in people and keeps them from discovering the joys that are intended for everyone. People who do not have the advantage of productive thinking will find themselves with a deformed attitude concerning life. It is based on ignorance and doubt. Positive and productive/constructive thinking is based on understanding and faith.

Your attitude determines a great part of your success. Technical knowledge is necessary, but it isn't everything. The most outstanding quality about anyone is his attitude. For every negative feeling that holds you back, you have a stronger, positive and constructive/productive one that can push you forward. Practice calling on your positive feelings and you will progress.

There comes a time in every person's life when he or she must wake up and rebel against the shallow demands of society and become the person he or she is capable of being. You can imprison yourself

Step VIII – Possibility Thinking

with nonproductive thoughts. Don't be like everyone else in the mediocre society. **Dare to be different. Dare to live your dream. You can, when you believe you can. It's up to you!**

Since you are allowed to choose whether to think nonproductively or productively, you determine your own destiny. Failure or success is your choice! Realizing this, you can develop the habit of succeeding by channeling your thinking! *This is the secret of the ages.* Great individuals have spelled it out for you. Will you continue to be caught in the "mire" of mediocrity or climb above the crowd? Most people yield to the behavior and thinking of others instead of thinking for themselves and controlling their own minds. Remember the law of the ages, simply stated, that we become what we think.

Marcus Aurelius said, "Our life is what our thoughts make it."

William James said, "The greatest discovery of my generation is that men or women can alter their lives by altering their attitude of mind."

The key to happiness, to success and to life, has been stated in many ways by many people. Everything that has been said is just a modification of a basic truth which has always been with us.

You can be great too, *if you decide to be*. Direct your thinking. Choose to think positively and productively. Become the person you want to be. Tell yourself over and over, "I become what I think of." What are you thinking about? Is it constructive, productive, and pleasant? Does it contribute to your success? This is what you must decide here and now. Will it be failure or success? The choice is up to you.

The right mental attitude will harmonize your total thinking. This productive/constructive/positive thinking can be the shortcut to your worthwhile purpose, so vital in every successful person's life. You will succeed when you think you can.

To succeed and alter your life's destiny, you must make a habit of possibility thinking. It will not be easy since we live in a world that is basically nonproductive. Ninety-five percent of the people are nonproductive. In other words, if you came up with a good idea, you would probably have to talk to one hundred people to get only five to encourage you to proceed with it. Almost everyone you know can always find something wrong with anything. People do not believe in

The Living Dreamer

the productive side of life. Nonproductive thinking becomes a way out, and progress is automatically hampered.

In a church that was far removed from the activities of any city, the people decided to vote on whether they would have a chandelier in the auditorium. One old man bitterly opposed it, and gave these reasons:
1. No one knows how to spell it.
2. No one knows how to play it.
3. Besides that, what we really needed is more lights!

Far too many people are like this old man. They are opposed to change in anything new or anything that they do not understand. This is the outgrowth of their nonproductive and negative patterns of thinking. They have already accepted a defeatist attitude towards life.

We have been endowed with the means to accomplish anything we can conceive that is worthwhile. Start today with a new outlook on life: one that is productive, that considers your possibilities for success. What a difference this makes! Turn your eyes toward success, not failure, and turn your back on disaster. Squash the fear of failure.

Possibility thinking is enhanced by:
Total Knowledge — Strive For It!!
Total Honesty   — Practice It!
Total Enthusiasm — Demonstrate It!
Total Commitment — Give It!

This new way of thinking is a tremendous attraction for good. It develops the best qualities in you and it draws the best from others. People like to be around those who have a positive command on life. You will become a leader instead of a follower!

When you can control your thinking and fill your mind with nonproductive thoughts, you will believe that any obstacle is too large to overcome. Reverse this and forget about failure! Act as though it's impossible to fail. You only have to be right fifty-one percent of the time to be successful!

Step VIII - Possibility Thinking

If you wait until everything is ideal for you to make it big, you will never begin. Stop listening to the ninety-five percent group. Most of the harm is done by people who do not know the facts. As you continue to strive for success, you may be criticized. Disregard this as coming from people who don't know the facts. Don't waste precious time and energy resenting it.

When you have made your decision to accomplish something worthwhile, don't change it. Keep yourself motivated by picturing the accomplishment of your goal. Only a small percentage of the people in this world can lead themselves. Recognize yourself for what you are and decide what you want to become and then *be that sort of person!*

Remember: We are worth exactly what we think we are worth.

Most of the people you know are too busy searching for excuses for their failures to find time to succeed.

Sometimes poor health can hamper one from striving, but more often it is a poor attitude that slows a person down.

Too many times we delay attempting something because we do not really believe it can be accomplished. We decide in advance that this task is not within our capabilities, so we leave it for someone else to do. Later we may find we are forced to attempt it, and quickly realize that what appeared impossible was easily completed. Often a victory or two is all that is needed to prove we can be victorious. Each productive victory encourages us forward.

A man was promoted to a national position where he was responsible for answering a large volume of mail. Fellow workers suggested that he cease writing his letters in longhand, and take advantage of a dictating machine. He was accustomed to organizing and reorganizing his thoughts by writing them down on paper. He took the negative approach and didn't bother attempting to learn to use the device. After many late hours at work, his wife suggested he try using the machine on short routine letters. He followed her suggestion and found it simple enough to do. Now he not only resorts to this added help for letters, but uses it for special instructions to his secretary, and even records conferences and phone calls with it. He now feels his work would be hampered without it.

The Living Dreamer

Use your fears and negative thinking as warning signs to bring your productive thinking to the rescue. Venture into the unknown. Enjoy the satisfaction of learning and doing something new. Don't worry about what your friends and neighbors will think. Forget it! Think for yourself. Think productively and positively. Remember that ninety-five percent of the people are going to disagree with you anyway. Why not be the pioneer, not the observer!

You possess greater possibilities than you've ever dared to believe. Remember, the average person only uses up to ten percent of their total mental capacity. In other words, for every dollar you are worth you have been spending only a dime! The most unexplored territory and the most fertile field in the world is on top of your shoulders! You really have what it takes to achieve great things.

When you are capable of reading and understanding these words, you can become a millionaire. When you believe in yourself and what you are capable of—you will succeed! Remember, you are who you are and where you are today, because that's what you really want. The choice was up to you and you made the decision. You can now make the decision to change who you are and start succeeding. But you must work to earn this gift that is lying dormant within you.

Many consider themselves either too young or too old to start their success journey. What is the right age? The "right age" is the age you are right now! There is no special age requirement for success, so forget about that aspect and start succeeding. You can think of a thousand reasons to fail, but you don't need one to succeed. Think of your mind like a parachute—it is only effective when it's open!

There was a picture of a turtle on a friend's wall. It said, "The only time the turtle makes progress is when it sticks its head out."

Most people are afraid to go out on a limb, when they haven't even started climbing the tree. But that is where the fruit is—out on the limb, not under the tree. Possibility thinking will help you climb the tree. The resulting self-confidence will send you out on the limb. If it breaks, just grab another on the way down, and use it to climb back up, even higher!

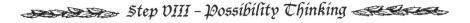

Step VIII - Possibility Thinking

"Life's battles don't always go to the
stronger or faster person,
But sooner or later, the person who wins is the person
who thinks he can!"

Your participation in the steps in this book is evidence of your desire to succeed. Now you owe it to yourself to follow through on the dreams that you have within, for they have been given to you for a reason.

The Living Dreamer

Come on!

Dare to bring your dreams into reality!

Step IX
Creative Imagination

reative imagination is our provision for the emergencies and necessities of life. Situations can be changed by this asset so they do not become problems. Creative imagination (or video-visualization) put in action by those who are above criticism, has been responsible for the progress of all civilization. Creative imagination opens the door to solutions even when the surrounding circumstances appear to make it impossible to be solved.

Everyone has his or her own unique powers of creative imagination, which can rescue anyone from the circumstances in life.

Here is what some famous people have said about the values of using the imagination:

- It develops courage.

    "I suffered terrible agonies of shyness as a boy. Sometimes I would walk up and down the embankment for twenty minutes or more before venturing to knock at the door. Few individuals have suffered more than I did in my youth from simple cowardice." — George Bernard Shaw

- It overcomes doubts.

    "Doubts are traitors and make us lose the good we oft might win by daring to attempt."—William Shakespeare

- It brings achievement.

    "There will always be dark days, but if your conviction of the value of the problem (situation) is such that you go right ahead in spite of the difficulties, the chances are you will achieve success in the end."—Charles Kettering

The Living Dreamer

"The more creative thinking we do, and the more ideas we give out, the more competent we become, and with this comes the most satisfying sense of accomplishment."—Carl Holmes

• It stimulates others.

"Ideas are generated best in an organization by friendliness. No stimulating, creative effort is so effective as a good pat on the back. We should do every thing possible to encourage people to get more better ideas."—Ernest Benger

There is a principle that you lose that which you are endowed unless you make use of it. The same principle applies to our gift, the imagination. It seeps out of our possession if we put it to no use. It grows even more valuable if we use it to work for us.

Here are some ways of increasing creativity through brain storming:

Brain storming means to use the brain to "storm," or attack a creative problem in commando fashion with each individual attacking the same objective.

• Rules for brain storming:
  - Criticism is not permissible. All nonproductive thinking is totally discouraged.
  - "Freewheeling" is welcomed, and the wilder the idea, the better. It is easier to tame down an idea than it is to "think up."
  - Combinations and improvement of ideas are sought out. Hitchhike on another person's idea. Group ideation is far more productive than individual ideation. One person can stimulate the thinking of others in the group.
  - Quantity is the goal. The greater the number of ideas, the more likely you are to come up with a winner.
  - Appoint a panel secretary to list all of the ideas. A panel chairman will edit the list and classify the ideas within logical classification. The ideas are then reported back to the group at a later time for further discussion and implementation.
• Practice acceptance of other people's ideas.

Step IX – Creative Imagination

Each brain storming session should be a game with plenty of rivalry, but with complete friendliness and acceptance all around.

- Establish a direction.

    Leo Nejelski said, "Meetings drift aimlessly when a clear statement of the problem is lacking. By stating the goal of the meeting, framework is established within which all thoughts can be directed."

    - Make a good start. "In the dim background of our mind, we know what we ought to be doing, but somehow, we cannot start. Every moment we expect the spell to break but it continues, pulse after pulse, and we float with it."—William James
    - Make notes. Keep these notes. Analyze them. When they get cold, look at them again.
    - Set deadlines and quotas for ideation.
    - Set a time and place that is conducive to good ideation. Make sure the group is compatible, since this is essential to good ideation.

- Research the problem thoroughly.

    "The process of research is to pull the problem apart into its different elements, a great many of which you already know about. When you get it pulled apart, you can work on the things you don't know about."—Charles Kettering

    "A problem well stated is half solved."—John Dewey

Humankind's mental functions can be simply stated as:
- Absorption: the ability to take in knowledge.
- Retention: the ability to retain and recall knowledge.
- Discernment: the ability to think logically.
- Imagination: the ability to think creatively.

Machines have been able to handle many of humankind's problems but cannot take the place of our creativity. Perhaps this is the basis for Albert Einstein's saying: "Imagination is more important than knowledge."

Here is how to develop your imagination:
1. Concentrate, or single-point focus. (Step II, Goals)

    Learn to trust your creative mind. Emile Coué (French

119

psychotherapist) said: "The subconscious mind simply will not take the trouble to work for one who doesn't believe in it."

2. Control your moods.

Dr. Howard E. Fritz, a researcher for B.F. Goodrich Company, said, "To induce creative thinking we cannot dominate or threaten. Such methods will not and cannot inspire. Inspiration is and can be the product only of free Mankind."

Following World War II, Dr. Max E. Bretschger, one of America's most creative chemists, was sent to Germany to determine how far the Germans had advanced in chemical warfare preparation. German scientists have always been among the world's greatest scientists. It was expected that under the Nazi whip they would have been driven far beyond what our chemists had achieved. Dr. Bretschger said, "To our surprise we found that we had out-thought the German chemists." They had become so concerned about their own personal lives in the hands of Hitler, they could not drive their minds to get the most out of their imagination.

3. Practice Imagination.

Walt Disney advised us to look upon our imagination as mental muscles. Dr. Alexis Carrel said, "The more a muscle works the more it develops. Activity strengthens it instead of wearing it out. Like muscles and organs, intelligence and moral sense become atrophied for want of more exercise."

Professor H. A. Overstreet said, "The imagination can actually be stimulated into growth."

W. Sommerset Maugham said, "Imagination grows by exercise and, contrary to common belief, is more powerful in the mature that in the young."

Creative imagination fired these men to attempt the impossible. In this area they had no competition. They realized the greatest success comes in helping others. They have often remarked, "No one is a success until he or she has helped someone else to succeed."

Creative imagination finds ways to compensate for any lack of education, training or experience.

Step IX - Creative Imagination

It is an amazing discovery to learn how many of the world's marvels have been invented by people with little formal training.

Mr. Henry Ford had little formal schooling. He did have a tremendous amount of creative imagination, however, and this creativity took him to the very top in the automobile industry.

Mr. Ford never allowed his lack of formal education to be a handicap. Once when he was being heckled by a particularly obnoxious person about this lack, he replied that he didn't feel this was a disadvantage at all. He observed that he had a row of electric push-buttons hanging over his desk, and that when he wanted a question answered, he placed his finger on the right button and called in the right man to answer that question. He wanted to know why he should burden his mind with useless details when he had able men around him who could supply him with any information he needed.

Mr. Ford's friend, Thomas Edison, was another one who surrounded himself with able men through whom he expanded his abilities and his own mind power, school education or none.

Imagination Induces the Flow of Creativity

Creativity has three basic levels:

1. The first, and perhaps the most shallow of all three levels, is to rearrange the order of things that already exist. This is a form of creativity, but what men and women do with it is simply to use what has already been made by someone else. They take all of the elements and then put them in some kind of new order. This is comparable to the procedure of a child putting blocks together. It can be compared to an adult mixing sand, gravel, water, and cement and making concrete.

2. The second level of creativity, which is more complex than the first, is to make something new utilizing what already exists around you. However, this is the level with which most people operate when they are being creative. It adds a new dimension to creativity for it uses the mind to create from all of the factors not yet in

physical form. Scientists are talking about the possibility, given the right temperature and the right equipment and over a period of time, of being able to create life itself. Some people say these scientists are tampering with things of the intangible realm and should not be attempting this. Others feel that they are to be commended. If they can take certain processes and come up with live cells, this is a wonderful feat. It is not, however, in the deepest sense of creativity.

3. The third level of creativity is by far the greatest of all three. On this level, "something" is created from "nothing." It is creating something which lies in the imagination as an invisible physical form within the mind, and is brought into tangible form in a physical presence.

There are many ways to develop creative ability. It is an interesting fact that the true creative force of the genius is not found in the area of the five basic senses where you might guess it is to be found.

The five basic senses are sight, taste, touch, hearing and smell. Each of these react in different ways to creativity but none of the five areas is creative in itself. Since most people have developed the five basic senses rather well, they spend most of their time, certainly the waking hours, in this area of consciousness. They are not aware they have a vast field of strength and potential in the area of the subconscious. Therefore, we must go on to the sixth sense.

Look at some practical things you can do to help develop your sixth sense, and begin to move into the creative areas of your subconscious. Begin by developing a workable list:

1. Find a time/place of quiet. The best time to think and to reach into the subconscious is when you can truly find an area and a time that is conducive to good thinking. The body must be relaxed from the tensions of the day. For many people the best time is in the morning when the mind is fresh and rested.

2. Have a regular place to go when you let go. The very area itself will soon become conducive to making you ready for your mind's creativity. An area next to the office is not a place for good, creative thought. Go off by yourself where you can relax and allow the mind to move, to wander, and to reach.

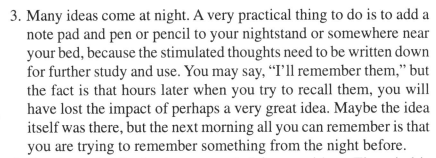

Step IX – Creative Imagination

3. Many ideas come at night. A very practical thing to do is to add a note pad and pen or pencil to your nightstand or somewhere near your bed, because the stimulated thoughts need to be written down for further study and use. You may say, "I'll remember them," but the fact is that hours later when you try to recall them, you will have lost the impact of perhaps a very great idea. Maybe the idea itself was there, but the next morning all you can remember is that you are trying to remember something from the night before.
4. Develop a habit of using your mind for new ideas. The mind is eager and ready at all times to explore all facets of the subconscious. You must help develop this very real habit daily by a constant reaching out to the subconscious mind.
5. Think in dimensions beyond those where you have been. Could there be a seventh sense, or an eighth, or a ninth? People are aware of the five basic senses because they are all conscious ones. Could there be five other areas of sensitivity in the subconscious? While thinking on these very questions, you cause your mind to begin reaching for dimensions beyond its normal use. Even more, when you begin to think on these things, you are causing your mind to expand.
6. Exercise and activate the mind. Think on other levels and of other ideas. For example: light travels at one hundred, eighty-six thousand miles per second. Therefore, it takes several seconds for the light from the moon to reach us almost instantly; your mind can go from here to the moon and back much quicker than even the speed of light. Think of humankind going to Mars. When we think of that possibility, that very thought becomes a possible reality. One day we will step on Mars, because prior to the event, humankind thought it could be done. Some people said we would never land on the moon, while others thought it could be done. We have done it. Creative imagination!
7. Creative imagination grows out of curiosity—*the ability to wonder.* "All philosophy," said Socrates, "began in wonder."

   The reason people are not willing to live like other animals is simply because they wonder. Something inside them tortured them with the desire to know. The desire to know is the incentive that enables humankind to keep up with life and to find out what it is all about.

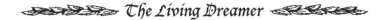

The Living Dreamer

The consciousness of the Highest Power is expressed in pictures drawn on the walls of caves of prehistoric humankind. And today, it is seen in the reflective symbols of all humankind.

In the field of science, curiosity is still greatly dynamic.

"The most beautiful thing we can experience is the mysterious," said Einstein. "It is the source of all true science."

It is this kind of wondering that leads people to far and distant places in their imagination. It is the great literature, great music, and great art.

One of the best ways to keep this curiosity alive is to listen to whatever happens to be going on around you each day. The one who works at this capacity to listen will hear the birds sing as they have never heard them before. They will hear music they did not know that before now had existed. They will be aware of "The Presence"—and the love in all humankind. This quality of listening has so much to give.

A probable cause of failure in many people is their inability to listen to the people who could open the way to discernment, and not hearing the voices in the many avenues they use to speak to all people.

There are two kinds of people in the world—those who follow their dreams, and those who don't. This inner voice cannot be explained, but it is there. *The important thing is to tune in on the right wave length and listen. . .*

This sense of wonder enables us to live beyond the moment in the hope of finding something more beautiful and meaningful in our lifetime. However, we will still need to obey the laws of society to save ourselves from the "jungle."

Humankind can never quit this game of life, as long as the sense of wonder flourishes. No one can go on fighting without inspiration. The source of all inspiration and motivation is related to curiosity. Life can seem a failure without something providing stamina and desire.

Lord Kelvin, a great scientist, achieved such success and recognition that a statue was erected to him in Glasgow, Scotland. This man said there was one word which characterized the most strenuous of the effort for the advancement of thermodynamics and electricity, that he

Step IX – Creative Imagination

had made perseveringly during fifty-five years. The word is failure. He was able to persevere in his creativity because something inside would not let him quit!

As you develop your creative imagination, you, too, become great! The more creative your imagination becomes, the greater your rewards will be.

Creativity is daring!

Step X
Stickability

Although this word is not found in the dictionary, "stickability" is a very real word. It is perhaps the greatest quality a person can have. For it is through a person's determination and capacity to stick to any task that makes them a successful achiever. Most people have automatic stickability when they are winning, but when they are not, they become apprehensive and quit. They not only cheat on themselves by accepting defeat as their "lot in life," they lose out on the happiness that could be theirs as well as the material things they deserve.

All of us have experienced not completing something. At the time we think we know why we are making the decision to quit. We try to justify the decision, find reasons why it wouldn't have worked out; making ourselves feel better about giving up. But we need to look at the real reasons why we quit, why we make a start but somehow just can't finish, to better understand ourselves and be successful. Understanding will help us remove the fear of failing, and it is only then that we will be able to develop the important quality of stickability.

It's all right to fail sometimes, as long as we have made an honest effort to succeed. We will learn things about ourselves that if we never made an attempt, we would never know whether or not it was meant for us. Once we can focus on why we give up, we'll be able to think more clearly and put all of our efforts into accomplishing what we want, and not give up at the first opportunity.

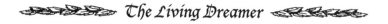 The Living Dreamer

Here are some of the reasons why we give up, and fail to accomplish what we want:
- fear of success
- lack of self-confidence
- habitual failure to follow through on what we start to its completion
- fear of failure and criticism
- not really wanting it in our life
- dwelling only on our past mistakes and not learning from them
- seeing ourselves as failures—thinking only negative thoughts about ourselves
- not being able to make decisions
- not believing that we're capable of being achievers
- trying to fulfill what someone else wants us to be
- not being able to motivate ourselves
- trying to achieve goals that are beyond our means to accomplish
- not being able to organize our time
- lack of resistance to anything in the way
- not asking for help or the assistance when we need it
- procrastination—putting things off until the last possible minute
- not making enough attempts, or not trying hard enough to succeed
- not researching all of the avenues and opportunities available to us
- not being able to take that first step, or finding out what that first step is
- not writing the steps down and concentrating on them with all of our energy every day

Remember: everything you desire must be written down! A daily journal is of vital importance. It is not only an excellent way to focus on what we want, but to see it in our own handwriting makes us acknowledge that we really want it. We then have a record of how we are doing, every day, and just how much effort we have been giving. This is a confidence-builder, a means to express ourselves and learn all we can about who we are. If we do not yet know where we want to go with our life, this journal can be our guide as to what is important to us, what we are interested in, what our abilities are, and give us some direction. It will give us the encouragement and incentive to keep going.

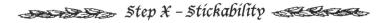

Step X - Stickability

Always keep in mind that every attempt is a possibility for success!

The trouble with most people today is that they fear criticism. Remember that all great men and women were criticized for their beliefs. If Columbus had not had the courage to accept criticism, he never would have sailed off to find America. History is full of examples of those who closed their ears to criticism—and they are the ones in the history books—not the critics! So why let fear of criticism or failure keep you from your purpose in life? Your life! How do you know you can't be successful until you make one or two more attempts? What you see as failure spurs others on to a greater effort!

Do you know that the difference in the average .250 hitter and the .300 hitter in the major leagues is just one more hit each 20 times at bat? But the difference in their salary is $30,000 a year!

Probably one of the best examples of stickability in the athletic world is in the New York Mets, who won the National League Pennant in 1969. The down-trodden victims of 737 defeats in seven years, the New York Mets were 100 to 1 shots. Yet they rose in splendor to defeat the Atlanta Braves in the play-offs of 1969 in three straight games.

The Mets went through years of ridicule that few teams have ever undergone. Yet in winning the World Series, they won the acclaim of the baseball world. Everyone seemed to think the players did not have the ability to build a team. Through determination, they built that team; and through rugged stickability they achieved success.

Everyone must have this same tremendous sense of determination if they are going to walk through all the barriers of life to achieve their desired success.

This principle will work for you in any endeavor in life. For it is simply from a lack of application and stickability that people fail in life. It has been said, "If there is anything that can be called genius, it consists chiefly in the ability to give attention to the subject which keeps it steady in the mind until we have surveyed it from all sides."

The Living Dreamer

Before you can realize your goals in life, you must first cultivate stickability. You will find this word the key ingredient in your climb to success. Since the dawn of history, every great person witnesses temporary defeat. Each had to ask themselves the same question that you must ask yourself. Ask yourself if you want failure to be your destination in life, or a temporary pause.

Stickability is the conviction of faith in yourself. All of us face this test of faith before we realize success. You deserve success, if you are willing to establish this conviction.

There are far too many people today boasting about what they could have been, had they been given a chance. A young man had a chance, in 1911, to invest an inherited $25,000 in a new company for five cents a share, but he was too smart. At least, this was his excuse for the fear of being criticized and the fear of failure. The name of the company was CocaCola. What would $25,000 at five cents a share been worth today?

We were born to dream, so why should we settle for less? Every fortune amassed in the world today was achieved with a recipe. True, there may have been thousands of different recipes used, but each one had at least two ingredients: first, there was an opportunity; second, stickability.

Henry Ford and his engineers failed, time and again, trying to invent the V-8 engine. And yet Henry Ford is remembered today for that feat: inventing the V-8 engine.

One of the most beloved and well-known leaders in the United States is Abraham Lincoln. But before he became president, Lincoln had endured eighteen failures. He continued to use stickability until he finally was elected President of the United States.

His story began over one hundred years ago. As a young man he grew up with an ambition to become a lawyer. He was not successful at law, so he tried to be a storekeeper and was unsuccessful at that. Then he became a surveyor, and the sheriff sold his equipment to pay the

Step X - Stickability

debts. He entered the army, and was not a good soldier. Hope entered his life, and then, ended, with the death of the woman he loved. He ran for public office several times, each time being defeated. He only succeeded one time in his life, and that was when he was 56 years of age. Today he is remembered not for all of the times he failed, but as a great emancipator and a great President of the United States.

Understand that a successful person is one who never quits. It's not a "lucky star" over their head. It's the individual's ability to stick with it—no matter what pops up along the way.

When those moments come (and they will!) when you feel it would be so much easier to let go—think stickability! Be like "super glue" to whatever it is you desire. It may only be right around the corner, with just a little more effort.

There are so many people that have a "wishbone" for a backbone. They only wish they had something; stickability is going ahead and doing it!

How to achieve stickability:

- Never, never, never give up or think defeat!
- Sustain faith in what you can be! Believe in yourself and what you can do.
- Make the decision to want to—right now! Let nothing steer you away from your commitment.
- Repetition, when you do something over and over and over, regardless of the outcome, you will master it!
- Determination: persevere until the realization of what you want— that desired goal— has been brought into physical form.
- Hold fast to that image of the final accomplishment—and don't let go of that image!
- Persist—do not let go, never say quit! Stick it out and never stop trying.
- Write down all of the obstacles in the way. If you can't remove them, then work around them!
- Once you have begun something, finish it to its completion, no matter what!

The Living Dreamer

Make a chart and place it on the wall at your home, office, anywhere you spend your time. First, write your purpose at the top of this chart. Next, draw a ladder without the rungs, and put your goal on the top. Make a ladder for each goal you want to achieve. Enter all of the opportunities and means that are available to reach that goal under each one. (This, of course, will take some extra effort on your part to research the avenues that are available and necessary to reach each individual goal.) Every day, look at each ladder, check off the items you have completed. Add items to each ladder if you have discovered more ways to obtain your goals. Remember, each rung is a test of your true convictions. Each goal you accomplish, each situation you encounter, is a rung on this "Ladder To Success." Look upon situations as opportunities to progress—by solving them.

Doing more than is expected of you—going the extra mile—means going past where others have stopped. It is your right as a "free person" to work as long and as hard as you like for your returns. Yet, most people never take advantage of this great right. However, it produces results (for you) and pays off (for you!). Success is measured by the amount of service you put forth, and your compensation is the rule by which this service is measured. Most successful people have been willing to go the extra mile, and it gives back more than can be imagined. It's like opening your own "bank" where your successes are compounded many, many times. So go for that extra mile and realize that it is actually the shortest way to reach your goals.

For every action there is an equal and opposite reaction; this is a Law of Physics, and it is also a Law of Life. There is no such thing as getting something for nothing; and what you give, you shall get the same in return.

You can achieve something great, but don't quit halfway. Many times you see the tragedy of people who could have achieved greatness, but who quit halfway. Their persistence gave way just as realization was about to come. It was out there, just beyond their outstretched fingers, but they were so tired—and let go. If they had just lunged for it one more time, they would have had it. When you get to the end of your rope, tie a knot in it and hang on!

Step X - Stickability

And why does one get tired and too discouraged? Well, maybe it's because of trying to go it alone. Try asking God (as you understand God to be) to help, to give you the strength and courage you need to stick to it, to keep at it. *And never give up! You will get help.*

These principles give you a formula for not being defeated by anything in this world. Nothing is impossible. You must believe this, and believe in "Infinite" help. You will find the strength and "know-how" to achieve the impossible. Remember, the easy thing about doing the impossible is that you have no competition! Very few believe they can or that you can, so try it!

Sometimes to prove your true belief and faith, you must turn loose of security and venture out. If you wait until everything is perfect before you get going, you probably will never start.

Make a promise to yourself—that you shall start doing more than is expected of you in everything you attempt. When you plant flower seeds, the more seeds you plant, nourish and take care of, the more flowers there are to bloom and become beautiful. This is also true about your future.

Remember: "Time is effort and effort is money."

In order to organize your time and become more efficient, consider following this procedure:

1. At night, write down in order of their importance, the most necessary tasks you are hoping to accomplish the following day.
2. Start working on the most important one, and when it is completed, cross it off your list and start on the second item.
3. Keep following your list, working at each task until it is completed.
4. If your list is not complete by the end of the day, put those items on your list for the next day.

Don't be concerned if you have only finished one or two tasks, as you will be working on the most important ones first.

This method will enable you to concentrate on what is most important to you and will teach you how to get the most out of each day. Do one thing at a time; stick with it until you achieve it; then go on to the next one in your order of importance.

The Living Dreamer

As you develop this quality of stickability, you will be amazed at the results! What will be even more exciting, is that you will discover that you have had this "power" within your reach all along!

What actually happens when we turn the power of stickability to any task:

1. Our inner mind begins to draw from the vast reservoir of all our past experiences to achieve what we desire.
2. We develop a kind of "mind-energy" that we didn't have before.
3. We develop enthusiasm for the desired subject.
4. We marshall the support of others to lead us to achieve this one particular thing.
5. We focus on the task and do not waste our inner energy, our physical efforts and our enthusiasm on inconsistent activities.
6. We develop a confidence that we did not have before—now we know we can achieve what we want.

Get enthusiastic about something and stick with it!

If you really want to be happy, set goals that command your thoughts, free your energies and inspire your hopes. Happiness is within. It comes from doing something into which you can eagerly put all of your strength, heart, thought, and energies. It also takes the *knowing when you are happy.* Sometimes we have to really focus on the fact that we are happy, that we do feel good about ourselves, for us to realize it. It doesn't just happen one day. *We make it happen.*

Alexander Graham Bell said, "Know what you want to do and go after it. The young man who gets ahead must decide for himself what he wishes to do. From his own taste, his own enthusiasm, he must get the motive and the inspiration which will start him on his way to a successful life."

Theodore Roosevelt said, "We've got but one life here. It pays, no matter what comes after, to try to do things, to accomplish things in this life, and not merely to have a soft and pleasant time."

C. W. Wendle said, "Success in life is a matter not so much of talent and opportunity, as concentration and perseverance."

Step X – Stickability

Through the power of stickability—staying consistently on achieving your chief purpose in life—you'll find amazing, fantastic abilities that you didn't know you have.

The Living Dreamer

Stickability is the power
to achieve success.

Stickability is the way to success!

Step XI
Explosive Enthusiasm

nthusiasm is one of the most contagious of all emotions. It doesn't matter who it comes in contact with—presidents, governors, educators, outstanding business executives, business associates, entertainers, farmers, or casual acquaintances—everyone comes away from its presence lifted by its tremendous explosiveness.

Enthusiasm comes from within you. It radiates outwardly in every expression of the face and every level of the voice, acting as a magnetic force to draw others to you. It is the "elan vital," which gives power, force and inspiration to everything you do or say. Enthusiasm is a beautiful state of mind that gains for you the cooperation of others, attracting them in a very positive way to your way of thinking and being.

Now that you have determined your worthwhile purpose and are on your way to achieving it through a progressive advancement of goals and possibility thinking, the world will soon realize that you are an adventurer, by your own display of enthusiasm. There is every reason for this display; every reason for you to be excited. Life is no longer a bore. Every day, every hour, every minute, there is a new and exhilarated meaning unfolding for you as a very unique individual. You know you are on the right track, and soon you will be enjoying the first of the "fruits of success."

Enthusiasm brings an air of excitement into everything you do. It causes you to glow with a radiant feeling of expectancy. It is the punch which delivers your message to others, making you soar in their estimation of who you are, and of who you are becoming.

No one completely lacks enthusiasm; the seeds of enthusiasm are within. You can let the seeds grow or you can smother them in negative thought and despair. The only limiting aspects are in your

The Living Dreamer

negligence to "water the seeds" with belief, love, encouragement, and opportunity. Enthusiasm is a great power within you, begging to be turned loose. Let it out! Don't be afraid to get excited. Don't be afraid to be different. You have the ability to control and channel the direction of your enthusiasm.

Enthusiasm can lead you aloft. It is your greatest asset, when put into action. Enthusiasm is hard to stop, once given freedom. You don't need more enthusiasm, rather you need to eliminate the negative thinking that weighs down the enthusiasm you now have.

The greatest damper to your enthusiasm is the feeling you do not deserve what you desire. Many people feel they were not meant to excel. Feelings of personal unworthiness are crippling and false. Your mind tends to prevent you from accepting great things until you have expended great effort. If you are not willing to pay the price for what you want, change what you want. You certainly deserve whatever it is that you are willing to seek and work for. Tell yourself you deserve it, and the subsequent release of enthusiasm will go about to achieve it for you. Once enthusiasm becomes the "inner spring of your joy, your life, and your motivation, it will not forsake you."

Always remember: Enthusiasm pours from the Infinite; you must keep in contact with it!

Sometimes people who fail pretend they are not interested in succeeding. If this applies to you, then stop pretending and start succeeding!

Every successful person must have enthusiasm. It is not a luxury ingredient, but an absolute necessity. When all else seems to fail, enthusiasm, prayer and hope cling together and push you through.

Once enthusiasm is released, it is like a fire—it always attracts attention. Anything you say or do, if not said or done with enthusiasm, is likely to bring little or no results. If the same words are said or done enthusiastically, it will get tremendous results. People respond to enthusiasm faster than to any other emotion. It is an inner belief put in action, and it radiates outwardly in every expression of the face and in every level of the voice.

Step XI – Explosive Enthusiasm

How many times have you heard someone say, "I enjoyed meeting him/her. They're so enthusiastic!" That person made an impact, because he or she expressed external zeal. Although perhaps not the most knowledgeable or professional person, that person wins with a "spark." Enthusiasm sells. People respond to it. It is a tragedy that so few possess enthusiasm. It makes the difference between a winner and a loser.

No one should miss expressing enthusiasm in every venture. But you need to make the distinction between enthusiasm and other emotions. There is a great difference between an inspired feeling and an animated feeling. The latter can be temporarily captured at a pep-rally or an exciting meeting. It is turned off and on and can be quickly lost. An animated feeling can be brought on by outward circumstances, but enthusiasm comes from within oneself.

Enthusiasm, more than any other emotion, also has a faster way of awakening and arousing the mind to action. When put into action, the mind is one of the most powerful forces known to humankind. Once your mind has received your message, it will quickly go to work to see that you attain your desire. But remember that this desire must be a purposeful one. For the more enthusiastic and the keener the desire, the sooner its fulfillment will materialize.

Remember: *everyone has the seeds of enthusiasm within.* However, these seeds must be nurtured and cultivated by your own determination. Enthusiasm doesn't simply spring "full blown." If you wait for someone else to bring it out, or for circumstances to justify your enthusiasm, you might have a long wait. You must make your own conditions, deliberately and systematically every day about everyday situations—the laugh of a child, the colors of a rainbow, the glow of a sunset, any number of things you come into contact with constantly. *Just open your eyes and your ears!*

Another way to build your enthusiasm is to think about your goals daily. Check up on your achievements and progress. Encourage those little sparks that flash upon you and get you interested or excited. Keep yourself alive and vibrant with enthusiasm.

Once you start practicing enthusiasm, it will grow by leaps and bounds. Soon you will find you are no longer consciously practicing it. It will simply be there, and it will be there at all times.

The Living Dreamer

People will know it and recognize it. You will be on your way to realizing your every dream. Others will get the impression you are ready and willing to invest in life and in yourself, and they will be ready and willing to invest in you, too.

Emerson said, "The world makes way for a man/woman who knows where he/she is going."

There is also a statement which says, "True happiness comes, not in doing what one likes, but in liking what one has to do."

There is no greater lesson to be learned in life than that of learning to do each job, no matter how distasteful of a job it is, and bring it to a successful conclusion. All those little tedious and mediocre jobs which have to be done in order to gain the ultimate goal, if done with enthusiasm, become not so tedious and mediocre. Each job, well done, is a lesson learned; and each of these lessons learned takes you a step closer to your goals.

Some people want to make the world over; some are impatient with the little jobs and are unwilling to bother with them. And still others want to hide from the world. The people who only want the big, important jobs that will bring them recognition and success, don't seem to comprehend that these same dull "little" jobs lead eventually to the big, important ones and ultimately to the very success and recognition they desire!

Enthusiasm adds one other dimension to all technical knowledge and professional skill—it can boost you on when in an atmosphere of defeat, and put you on the mountain top of achievement, unity, and love. It tramples over prejudice and opposition, creates action, and hurdles all obstacles. The power within your mind comes alive and you become an individual of action. **Simply stated, your achievements are always in direct proportion to your degree of enthusiasm.**

Enthusiasm is shown on your face. One of Abraham Lincoln's advisors urgently recommended a candidate for appointment to Lincoln's Cabinet. The President declined. When asked why, he replied, "I don't like his face." The advisor retorted that the man was not responsible for his face. President Lincoln said, "Everyone is responsible for their face after they're forty."

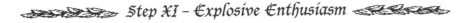

Step XI - Explosive Enthusiasm

Enthusiasm attracts attention. People who are enthusiastic proclaim to the world by their actions and in their countenance, that they have what it takes to get to where they want to go. There is nothing more attractive than an animated face and bright personality. Such a person attracts success. Display of excitement shows interest, conviction and self-confidence.

Enthusiasm has the same relationship to humankind that fire bears to a steam boiler. It heats up the powers of the mind and gives you the necessary force of action. Search out worthwhile work. Get excited about it! Discover success!

Enthusiasm must be kept at a high level and maintained. To do this in relation to any particular task, you must keep repeating the task or project until you build enough self-confidence to sail into the job.

When you are feeling low and enthusiasm is hard to generate, expose yourself to excitement. Releasing your enthusiasm will help you climb out of mediocrity or a rut. You will become a dynamic individual, and your self-confidence will grow. It will not only grow within you, but it will reach out to others and lift them from apathy and lack of concern.

Every brain is a "broadcasting and receiving station" for thoughts and attitudes. Enthusiasm is an intense emotion and penetrates the minds of all who come within its range. **Everyone reveals the true nature of their thoughts without realizing it.**

Since you will be developing in the same way you think, then think enthusiastically. Your persistent enthusiasm will win results. Ralph Barton, the distinguished journalist, states that if he had one gift to give his son, he would give him enthusiasm!

Developing your enthusiasm is not easy—it is a challenge. This is probably why the majority is unenthusiastic; the majority will try to restrain you with confirmed pessimism. Don't be pessimistic—be optimistic! You must dare to be different, if you dare to dream.

Enthusiasm is probably the most important ingredient in your success adventure, and the most misunderstood word in the English dictionary. Only a few will recognize the genius in business and other fields of endeavor. These people step up the vibrations of their own minds through the capacity of their enthusiasm, until they are able to

The Living Dreamer

communicate with a source of knowledge, wisdom and creativity not available through the faculty of reason.

An author shows enthusiasm in every word, even though the work may be translated into many languages. The lawyer can have an innocent client, the best facts, the most conclusive evidence, and yet lose their case due to a lack of enthusiasm.

No job is ever dull to the one who is alive with action. How can you expect results without exhibiting excitement? Enthusiasm can make the difference between an effective speaker and a bore, action and laziness, success and failure.

Your mind is stimulated by your excitement. It will work for you if you provide the enthusiasm it thrives upon. Emerson said, "Nothing is so contagious as enthusiasm—it moves stones, and charms brutes—it is the genius of sincerity, and truth accomplishes no victories without it."

You will find that your advancement in your work will be in direct proportion to your display of enthusiasm. It radiates self-confidence, and attracts favorable attention. An enthusiastic individual cannot be held down. This is the type of person companies like to have around. Enthusiastic people, happy in their work, will influence others in this direction; and they are certainly more valuable than any expert with an unenthusiastic, nonproductive, negative attitude who will put down the attitude of everyone they associate with.

When a person lacks enthusiasm, it is evident. They publicize the fact of their weak response to life. Their tone of voice, posture, and self-confidence are all mediocre.

Thomas Edison did not lack enthusiasm. He endured approximately 10,000 failures before he perfected the incandescent electric lamp. He was inspired to his enduring enthusiasm, backed by his worthwhile purpose.

Of all the great American industrialists who contributed to the development of our industrial system, none was more spectacular than the late Walter Chrysler. Chrysler started as a mechanic in a railroad shop in Salt Lake City, Utah. When his

Step XI - Explosive Enthusiasm

savings reached $4,000 he made a decision to set himself up in business. After looking around, he decided the automobile was the coming industry and went into that field. First, he invested all his savings in an automobile. He proceeded to take the automobile apart, piece by piece, and then put it back together. He repeated this operation until he made his mind "automobile conscious." He observed every detail of the car, and soon knew all the good points and all the weak ones. He commenced to design automobiles, drawing from this experience, incorporating the good features and omitting the weak ones. He did his job so thoroughly that when the Chrysler automobiles reached the market, they became the sensation of the entire automobile industry. His rise to fame and fortune was rapid and definite, because he had desire and then the enthusiasm to make it a reality.

If you want to be an achiever, turn your enthusiasm loose and start "fanning your desire into white heat to create a burning desire."

Your burning desire will flourish on the enthusiasm you demonstrate as you work towards your accomplishment.

Guidelines for Enthusiasm:

1. Develop a great sense of expectancy. Every morning say, "This is a great day for work, happiness, sharing and caring."
2. Also begin the day with, "This is a day I will make, and I will love every second of it!"
3. Know and understand that you control your mind, thoughts and actions.
4. There is a law of Nature which makes your thoughts and habits permanent. So make them positive and productive.
5. Know that this same law conveys your thoughts to others.
6. Any state of mind is contagious. So make sure you have the right mental attitude.

143

7. Enthusiasm increases personal initiative and creates a more optimistic spirit.
8. Everywhere you go, reflect this productive attitude.
9. Build your personality with strong self-discipline, self-confidence, persistence, courage, ambition and a keen imagination.
10. Your personal appearance gives a picture of who you are and what your goals are.
11. Enthusiasm is the expression of hope, belief, understanding and unity of all things—Love. It builds unity, achievement and love in all people, everywhere. Enthusiasm must have action behind it.
12. Enthusiasm is the avenue to your mental growth and development.
13. Practicing the attainment of your purpose, serving humankind, belief, right mental attitude, burning desire, awareness of the studying of yourself to know *you,* pleasing personality, creative imagination, good human relations, selecting the highest values, learning from defeat, having the best of health, highest endeavors, and an honest searching to bring you a radiant and contagious enthusiasm.
14. Enthusiasm is the combination of mental, physical, and an inner energy. It is belief that is willingly put into action.

Believe in yourself!

Be enthusiastic about what you do!

And you will when you

Dare To Live Your Dream

Step XII
Producing Results

This is the final step, and yet it is perhaps the most important. Now, let the inspiration you feel and the information you have been receiving "skyrocket" you to even greater heights!

Your "track record" of the kind of results you produce is a direct reflection of your ability to organize your time and plan your work. An efficient, results-producing person has a tremendous T.N.T. rating: Today Not Tomorrow. Be the one who does things, not just talks about doing them. The person who wants to do something and is forever talking about it, actually never follows through on doing it.

You can drop the habit of procrastination right now. How? Get the job done today. Putting things off until tomorrow has been a major fault in all of us. Develop the habit of "Do it now!"

Benjamin Franklin asked, "Do you love life? Then do not squander time, for that is the stuff life is made up of."

And it was Kerr who said, "Live this day as if it were the last."

Have you ever seen anyone become entrapped in a revolving door which turned faster than they expected? It spins around a few times and they head off in the first available direction. This is exactly how many lives function. The people who have no plans for the use of their time, their life is like a revolving door or a merry-go-round. They never get anywhere. They are in a constant circle of repetition. Their outlook on life fluctuates like that of a wooden horse on a carousel, up and down, up and down. There never seems to be enough time to get things done, but there is always time available to waste. The job suffers, the family suffers, and there are nonproductive consequences.

The Living Dreamer

Producing results depends on the right use of time.

If your life seems to be spinning around in circles, jump off onto solid ground and take some time to think, study and plan. This time will be well spent, for it will help you find direction. You will begin to make headway, by planning the best use of your time for the best results. Time is money, health, and security. It is automatically progressing, never stopping. You need to plan your work in detail and be "hardheaded" about working your plan. Killing time is not murder; it is suicide. *Time wasted today can never be regained tomorrow.*

Begin now to develop your plan of action. Become frugal with time. Set aside time for your family, social life and religion, as well as your work. Balance your life and your time. Organize your day, your week, your month. Write down the things you want to accomplish. Schedule your work. Set target dates for completion. And most importantly, be sure everything is carried out!

Develop an "Important List" and an "Imperative List" for each day. List the things that must be accomplished that day, putting the most urgent item first. On the "Important List," write down the things that you would like to accomplish, time permitting. At the day's end, evaluate your Imperative and Important Lists. Any important items unaccomplished that have become urgent should be transferred to the Imperative List for the next day. Do not be overly concerned if you have only done the first few items on your list. You have done the most important ones. You are learning to think and plan your work according to that which is most important. This simple method of power planning will help you develop a habit of efficiency and will result in absolute inflexibility about obtaining them. This is the art of successful time planning.

Practice single-focusing and concentrating on one effort at a time. Don't split your talents and thinking, the result being inefficiency. Concentrate on the job at hand, finish it, and continue to stay on your established schedule.

Guard yourself against believing only you can perform a certain task where you work. Learn to delegate authority. If no one can replace you, how can you advance? Don't spend your valuable dollar time on

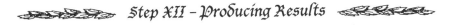

Step XII - Producing Results

penny jobs. Accomplish the important things first. No one really plans to fail, some just fail to plan.

Though some forms of daydreaming can bring positive results, it takes no brains. It also brings no results to fulfilling your ultimate purpose. You must eliminate the negative daydreaming.

Don't be lazy. Be active. Don't fall into the trap of providing excuses for procrastination. Take inventory. Take time to think. What is killing my time? Where am I wasting it? How can I become more productive?

Your life sometimes may seem like quicksand; you never get completely organized, with your feet planted on firm ground. But even quicksand can be changed.

Years ago, the Chase Manhattan Bank started excavation for a new skyscraper. Since most of Manhattan Island is made up of solid rock, it has been the foundation for many tall buildings. However, the land owned by the Chase Bank contained a large pocket of quicksand. The bank called in experts to find a way to meet the situation. One suggested pilings, another caissons, but the cost of these was prohibitive. Geologists were consulted on how long it would take to turn the quicksand into sandstone. About one million years was their reply. The bank felt they couldn't wait that long. They called in some soil solidification people. The people knew how to handle quicksand. They sent pipes down into the quicksand and pumped a solution of sodium silicate and calcium chloride into it. In a few days the quicksand solidified into sandstone, hard enough to permit the erection of a sixty-four floor skyscraper building.

If this seems like a miracle, it is nothing compared to the change that takes place in the human personality when a person applies the principles in *daring to dream*—when a person can shed the "chemicals" of defeat, habit and pessimism, and exchange them for achievement, fulfillment and purpose.

Organization of our time will produce results. It is a reflection of goal-setting. Time organization is a goal. You have a task and you complete it within a certain span of time.

The Living Dreamer

During World War II, when the submarine program was critical, delivery was set on tight schedules with dates for completion that seemed impossible. However, most of the dates were met, much to the surprise of the skeptics. A challenge had been sounded, an inner thought had been implanted, and the job was completed on time. Goal setting paid off! The impossible accomplishment became the possible result.

Get yourself and the day started right away.

Have you ever noticed that when you wake up a little early in the morning, that you poke around, not really doing much? Knowing that you have a little extra time tends to make you ease up. Actually, it is a form of inefficiency and a lack of self-discipline. Wouldn't it be better to arrive at the job a little early and clean up a few details before the activity begins, or maybe think of a couple of things that need your attention at home?

Plan to rise early. Get just the amount of sleep required (for you). Don't get a slow start. Jump into your work! You can save time by delegating menial tasks and eliminating casual conversation. When you are busy, others will not take your valuable time. Learn to cut corners where advisable. Don't waste time, treasure it. The sand in your hourglass gets lower and lower, whether you waste it or not.

You should make it a point to control your work. Get organized.

Put everything in its proper place. The foundation for all work is good order and planning. Eliminate distractions. Make yourself less accessible to the routine office traffic. There are too many inefficient individuals who want to justify their loss of efficiency by decreasing yours! To plan adequately, you must decide on what it is you are going to have and do, and then make it happen.

No compromise is permissible. No excuse or rationalization is acceptable when you are willing to pay the price. You must ask yourself if the rewards in your work are worthwhile and important enough to you and your family to deserve your best efforts. Is your sacrifice worth the price? Or should more time be spent with the family? Should you contemplate more desirable work? Whatever your answer is, you

148

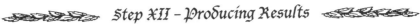

Step XII - Producing Results

must realize that you are responsible for destroying any barriers. Reading good, productive books, associating with people who are improving themselves and being alert to the possibilities in life, open doors for you to become a greater individual.

One person who has gained help from the principles in this book wrote: "For the first time in my life I can see where I have created my own bad luck by my thought patterns. Since reading your book, I have become aware of hostility, resentments and other barriers to my being a happy and resourceful person. I realized how silly it was to carry these restrictions around in my system. I was truly my own worst enemy. My pattern of failure and defeat has been changed to the way of *The Living Dreamer*. This is a new way of life and a movement in which I am glad to have a part. I feel I have given myself plenty of opportunities, but I was blind. Now I see them."

Be the most attractive and productive person you can be!

It will serve you well to attract more friends, to develop productive habits, and to make the most use of your time. Keep your time purposeful and your purpose clear. Make decisions, because indecision and the lack of a definite purpose are the greatest thieves of time. A person who can make up his or her mind has the power and the will to become a leader.

The ability to make decisions is lacking in many people. They are in conflict, full of doubts, and they fear failure. This type of thinking is a good indication that they lack self-confidence.

People have become too "security conscious." Society conditions us to be careful, cautious, think things over, not act hastily and to get advice. Does this sound familiar? This is fine if you want to conform, but any person who can make a fast decision is a winner.

Success demands you to be an adventurer. Most people find themselves running from life's decisions instead of stopping and facing them head on. Don't waste time by allowing yourself to become bogged down with indecision. At first some of your decisions may be wrong—but don't be afraid of being wrong sometimes. The more you practice

The Living Dreamer

making decisions, the more you will find that they are the right ones, and the less afraid you will be of making them. So when in doubt, make a decision and go forward with it.

Get a "kick" out of every day. Make life more adventurous. Plan your life by planning your goals. Enrich your life. Begin a life of action right now. An aggressive man, woman or child never holds back reserve strength. Too many people restrain their powers for a better time or a brighter-looking opportunity. They know they can achieve more than they do, but they think, "Just wait until the right break comes along and watch me fly into action!" This type of thinking won't even get you off the ground floor! The individual of real action will put every ounce of energy into their efforts for the present conditions. They make the circumstances. They do not believe in chance or luck. To develop more energy, they merely translate their thoughts into forward movement.

Produce results by making each day count.

Instead of thinking that you have "problems"—think of them as being "situations." Forget the word problem and refer to these barriers as situations. A situation can be magnified into a problem only by your mind's attitude. *Always remember that there is no problem greater than its solution.* Your "used-to-be" problems are only temporary situations. The best way to handle your situations is by handling them one at a time. And always think of your situations as being in the present tense, and solve the one at hand.

Take the following steps when solving a situation which requires a definite decision:

1. Write it down—define it. Usually a situation defined is half-resolved or at least reduced in importance.
2. Analyze the situation—study it.
3. List the alternate solutions in the best order of application.
4. Ask the necessary and important questions—who does it help? And who does it hurt? It may help you, but it may hurt someone else even more.

150

Step XII - Producing Results

5. Now ask: Are the answers to the above questions a result of ambition wherein you are willing to pay the price, or of greediness wherein you are looking for something for nothing?
6. Picture the consequences of your decision, and then ask yourself if you can live with it.
7. It is all right to obtain advice, but be sure that your decision is your own.
8. Once you have made your decision, stick to it as if you were unalterably stuck with it. Do not change your decision unless new facts can be presented to warrant a change.
9. Put your decision into action. Employ every power available in carrying out your decision. *Make it work!*

When some plan of action works for you, double its use. When it fails, revise it. Pay attention to your plan. Success requires you to be a man or woman who knows what he or she is in command of. When you hear the voice of doubt whisper, "It's beyond your power," whisper back, "You just think so!" Do this even if at the time it doesn't make sense, and soon the reason will become clear. You shouldn't compromise with what you want. Plan, act, know that you may make a few mistakes, revise your plans and don't settle for less than your goals. Pay attention to your goals because paying attention pays.

Constantly act upon whatever you know to be the best action at the time. Become known as an individual of action. Come alive by producing results. Ask yourself, "What could I become if nothing were in my way?" Act as though nothing is in your way, and you will find it to be the truth.

Keep your goals and plans out in the open with enthusiasm and self-motivation. Time is on your side, but it is an excuse for a majority of the people. Successfully organized people use time as their servant instead of their master. The unsuccessful ones do not lack time, they lack self confidence, self-command, and action. Don't allow indecision and procrastination to slow you down and kill your time! Make bold plans, but don't wait for tomorrow to carry them out—act now! You can gain time only by cutting out unnecessary time

killers. Discontinue following your usual course and compel yourself to change direction. Don't follow the follower; you be the leader,
you set the pace!

You know time never stops. If you live to be seventy-five
years of age, you are "allocated" 657,450 hours. But, remember,
you only have 24 hours in one day to spend. If you require six to
eight hours of sleep, you will be left with only about 438,300 hours
of achievement time. Therefore, you should learn to invest time
instead of spending it. *Manage your time.* Put more energy into
your efforts so your investment of time will reap dividends instead of depreciation.

Strive to get the most from your latent abilities and from your inner mind.

You can accomplish so much more when you realize and
accept a simple truth about the latent abilities of your inner mind.
For only when it is understood and appreciated can the use of
the inner mind be very effective. It contains the power to create,
and it will "obey orders" that it is given by the conscious mind.
It is a known and proven scientific fact that when an order is
given to the inner mind, the mind acts efficiently and accurately
to obey that order. Give your desires, plans and goals to your
inner mind and it will follow through with creative action to fulfill them. The inner mind is like a total storehouse and it is filled
with knowledge and energy. It is also known as the active file of
the mind. It never grows tired and is at your disposal constantly.
State precisely whatever it is you desire to accomplish, and then
watch it happen!

To accomplish your plan you must organize your time. And time
is money. To the person who earns $10,000 a year, time is worth $5.00
an hour; while the one who makes $20,000 a year has time valued at
$10.00 an hour.

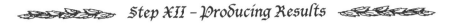

Step XII – Producing Results

You have been guided through these steps, and have been awakened to a greater meaning of your life and to the joy of living.

No one is truly living up to his or her capacities and potential. The first challenge in your adventure was to have a definite purpose for your life—a vital, worthwhile purpose. Any person who is not fulfilling a purpose is like a ship without a rudder. They are tossed upon the ocean without any hope of reaching a "Port of Destiny"—without ever realizing a sense of having been created for something special.

No life is without purpose. The Creator does not disdain anyone. Everyone is someone in Its sight. It has a purpose for every body and every mind. **You must believe your thoughts can and will come true, NOW!** This is faith at work! Always maintain the prevalent hope that something good is going to happen to you. That which the mind can conceive and believe, it can then achieve. You can be free from the bondage of mediocrity.

At this stage of your journey you have formed your own personal concept of what you consider success. Are you receiving the income you desire? You and your family are entitled to a good living and life's abundance. Under material possessions you might have listed a luxurious home, beautiful furniture, a fine car, nice clothes, hunting or fishing equipment. Under "physical being" you probably want health, happiness, control of emotions, and peace of mind.

Certainly, you should want to add spiritual goals. You might have listed Universal Love—reaching out to everyone, when it is genuine, from all to all with complete unity, the understanding of all things, and to the person that you are attached to. There is respect, dedication, and commitment to a cause one can reach, together with someone, or by oneself.

Yes, the key to your success is to find your own power of purpose. What is the difference between one person and another? Is it the mind? Many think so. Research has shown that the difference in a genius and an "ordinary" person is the desire to learn, the constant search for knowledge, and the capacity to apply wisdom.

There is no way to keep a purposeful individual down. Throw him in a hole and he will make a ditch out of it and sell the dirt for gardens.

The Living Dreamer

Clarence E. Birdseye lost all of his money—all he ever had, even the money borrowed on his insurance—when his frozen food business failed. He still believed there was a market for frozen food. He started over with seven dollars ($7.00!) and borrowed a corner of a friend's ice plant for his experiments. Five years later, his seven dollars had skyrocketed to $22,000,000! This did not seem to completely satisfy his purpose. He then went on to secure more than two hundred and fifty patents in the United States and foreign countries. He developed many new ideas in the food processing field.

H. V. Kaltenborn quit high school after one year, moved from one job to another as a worker in a lumber camp, a door-to-door salesman, and a war correspondent. Then, having only attended one year of high school, he went to Harvard and graduated cum laude. He became the most widely known voice of World War II. Why? Because he was a man with a powerful purpose.

Those who have purpose in their lives never cease achieving. There is a power within them that wipes away all indifference, laziness, or lack of ambition. They know anyone who has succeeded in life has had bad starts and difficult times. They're prepared for struggles before they arrive, but they never lose heart. They have been introduced to their better selves—the new self—for the rest of their lives. And that means they are living in prosperity.

Consider some of the inspirational figures of the past:

John Bunyon is noted for a "Pilgrim's Progress," one of the finest pieces of all English literature. Bunyon was imprisoned and punished severely for his viewpoints. He would not go along with the "status quo." It was when he was in prison that he was introduced to his better self and wrote his great masterpiece.

The noted Charles Dickens was making a living by pasting labels on blacking pots. He had been through a tragic love affair which had penetrated his soul, and brought him into the depths of despair. Out of the tragedy in his life came the wonderful books loved by all

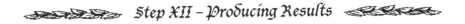

Step XII - Producing Results

generations. It was the heartache resulting from this deep love that produced David Copperfield.

The poet Robert Burns, an illiterate country lad, was born in poverty and grew to become a drunkard. He began to clothe his beautiful thoughts in poetry and removed the thorn in his flesh, to plant a rose.

Beethoven was deaf but was able to compose the glorious symphonies that have enthralled the entire world for centuries. How could a musician write such music and not hear it? He listened within himself—with a sense of hearing beyond the ordinary sense. His definite purpose found a way where others might have given up.

Milton was blind but he was able to transform his dreams and thoughts so that everyone could see into his heart. His descriptive words seemed to come from one who had eyes to see all of the beauty of all living creations and earth.

O. Henry discovered the genius lying dormant within him when he was confined to a prison in Columbus, Ohio. It was there that he was forced to discover his "other" self. He began to use his prolific imagination to write short stories and thereby added to the wealth of literature.

Helen Keller became deaf, dumb and blind shortly after birth, but this misfortune did not keep her from being one of the great figures of history. Her entire life has served as evidence that no one is defeated until defeat has been accepted as a reality.

Mme. Ernestine Schumann-Heink was told, in her first interview with a professional musician, that she would never be able to sing. She stood before the master teacher, an awkward, poorly dressed girl. This man said to her very abruptly, "With such a face and with no personality at all, how can you ever expect to succeed in opera? My good child, give up the idea. You can never be a singer." But something within her would not give up. This man knew little about what it takes to produce

155

results if a person has a definite purpose, goals, and a beautiful, heart-felt desire. This awkward girl had a desire and the determination to see it through. She became a woman the world still acclaims with the greatest of them all.

It has been suggested earlier that you write down your desires and what you want to accomplish in life. The more you dedicate yourself to those accomplishments, the more they will become yours—one day to have and to hold. The more complete the process of growth takes place within you, the more you will become the person you've always dreamed of being. And the more you trust in this process, the more it will change you from who you present yourself to be on the "outside" to who you are on the "inside."

When desire is backed by faith, it releases a power within that will lift us from "lowly beginnings" to places of influence, affluence, happiness and health.

When our desire has been backed by our faith and our belief that we deserve whatever it is that we desire, our lives are then transformed and uplifted to a life that is on a "higher level" than where we are living presently. When we can drop the word "if" (as you have learned to do) we can head toward our goals.

Producing results will involve you in your community and will inspire you to help others.

Andrew Carnegie's dreams of success always seemed to involve helping others. Before, and even after he became a multimillionaire, he was constantly involved in the community. Through him and his research program, millions of people have been inspired to attempt a greater way of life.

Our definite purpose will keep us on the right course. It is like a magnet that draws from all sources of the conscious and the subcon-

Step XII - Producing Results

scious, or inner mind, to bring our purpose and desires into reality. Purpose inspires us to heights we have not yet reached and joys of fulfillment we have not yet experienced.

Goals are like the mileposts strung along the planets as we make our astronomical rise to the galaxies. Goals turn on the light for us to see the way to the next step, and to enjoy our next adventure to success.

Each day of your life can be enhanced and enriched by planning goals. When circumstances develop for the realization of these goals, don't be caught unprepared. When opportunity knocks at the front door, most people are out in the backyard looking for four-leaf clovers!

List six objectives for each day in the order of their importance. Don't be disappointed if some are not completed, for you will be doing the most important ones.

A burning desire will ignite you. Picture it as the fuel in a rocket that blasts you off of the launching pad. Whatever a person can conceive mentally, his or her own burning desire will create the motivation for it to materialize in reality.

Self-discipline is the most important requirement for individual success. Without self-discipline, nothing will "fall into place." Self-discipline means taking possession of your mind with such strength that your emotions, instincts, thoughts, and body are under your complete control.

Your relationships with people will improve; they will take on greater significance *because you are a more significant person.* Remember that you interpret and judge others by who and what you are. You look at the world from your own viewpoint and your own aspirations, and will relate to others and the outside world by who you are inside.

Possibility thinking will eliminate the nonproductive and accentuate the productive. You are going to be so much happier and freer from the bondage of the past, for you will be living in the joys of the present. An adjusted system of Nature acts as a productive stimulus to a happy, worthwhile, and meaningful life. Life will never be the same for you. Everything will be different because you will be different totally and completely. A built-in awareness of the systems of Nature that you have had since you were conceived has now created the path that will reach the stars.

The Living Dreamer

Creative imagination—utilizing our video-visualization capabilities—launches our potential greatness to such magnitude that we are amazed at who we are and who we are becoming. The beginning of our world is described in terms of creating the earth and all of its inhabitants from absolutely nothing but a Word. This is also an accurate description of the power of our own creative imagination. We begin this same kind of process by creating our way to success and fulfillment from absolutely nothing in physical form within our own mind.

Explosive enthusiasm will always take us higher. It will add dimensions to our lives and to any group of people gathered together. They will emerge into those who can never be satisfied without fulfilling their own destiny.

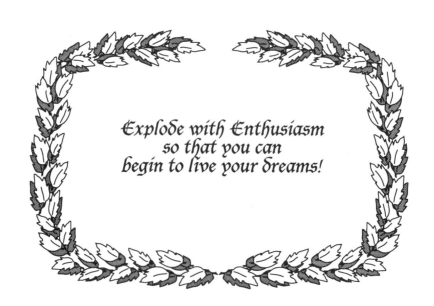

Explode with Enthusiasm so that you can begin to live your dreams!

Flying in a Dream

he Living Dreamer is a mind flight toward understanding the motion of a dreamer moving toward achievement and success. I want you to know that you are the dream of all dreams. You prosper above all mountain peaks of your impossibilities. You will now achieve the unknown spheres of failures and make them successes. You now have the tools to go out into a make-believe world that you have been told treats you unfairly and make it a masterpiece of dreams and untold stories of your achievements. I will leave you with this, and with this you shall become the dream. Keep it with you always. Engrave this poem in your mind and act upon it. I believe in you. Become your dream.

I speak unto all dreamers:

You have found your own purpose in life,
   and you know what it is...

You are a seeker of the secrets in you,
   and you are learning what they are...

You are a seeker of inner wisdom,
   and you know what you seek...

You are a seeker of inner knowledge,
   and you know what it is you seek...

And you have learned how to fly,
   and the desire to do it again...

You have a map of success,
   and you know the way...

The Living Dreamer

I know now that you know. You just needed some directions and a map to get there. I hope that this generation and generations yet to come will accomplish the impossible with what has been given within these pages and what will be learned by applying them. You have been guided in the best way possible to your own yellow brick road. Now, it is your turn to walk to your dream over the hill. But, I will be there watching you make it over that hill. And if you stray away from the path just a little bit, there will be that inner dreamer's voice echoing out to you that will help you find your way back on course and remembering how to *live your dream.*"

And remember:

Your enthusiasm energizes every part of you, and keeps regenerating once you take that first step. If ever you need replenishing, close your eyes. Let the contents of this book fill your mind—let the words encourage you just as a friend would. For all dreamers are with you in thought, and are with you as you read the words within these pages. You can change your life by these words and by applying them to your life. Everyone can. But it is up to each individual to take one's life into one's own hands, and to pursue the dreams that live within the imagination. These dreams have been given to each individual for a reason. And even though our dreams have been given to us free of charge, it is up to each of us to bring them into the tangible world around us.

The knowledge that you now have can be spread everywhere and, like wildflowers, grow in abundance for all to enjoy. Let your self-improved life be an example for others. And when someone asks you how they can achieve success in their life, just smile and say,

Dare to live your dream and the dream you'll be!"

B. Angelson

Become Your Dream

Yes, it is time to spread your wings and fly to the destinations that are waiting just for you. I have found my wings of flight, and I know it can be done. I come from very humble beginnings, and yet I am soaring towards a new world that I have been creating. I am becoming the one I have envisioned within my mind and know I was born to be. It will take time for everything to be in place, for the spiral of individual creation to reach its aspirations. But the vision is crystal clear.

It takes persistence; following through on opportunities and insights that come my way. I ventured into the unknown. And I came to know someone I did not know could exist on this earth nor in this life. I thought it was just a dream, an apparition that came to me only as if to entertain and comfort. I pursued with new-found courage and, when I looked deeper into the image in my mind's eye, I realized that the being I was looking at and contemplating with love and admiration— was my inner self—the bare Soul expressing its Divine Purpose: freedom of being.

Now, it is your turn. The knowledge and understanding within the pages of this book are here to help you find your true self. And this is the person you were created to become and will become. Don't be afraid to dream. It is a gift. Accept it. Open it. Use it. And Love It.

Nothing will give you a greater feeling than knowing you are on your way to fulfilling a destiny that has been yours from the moment you were created.

Believe, and it will happen in your life as it has happened in mine...

The Living Dreamer

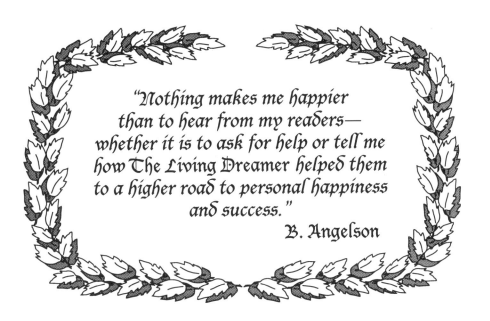

"Nothing makes me happier than to hear from my readers— whether it is to ask for help or tell me how The Living Dreamer helped them to a higher road to personal happiness and success."

B. Angelson

For corporate training and educational information:
Feel free to write to B. Angelson when you have a question.
Any message addressed to the author can be sent to:
B. Angelson & Associates
PO Box 236
Kent, WA 98035
(206) 859-1714
(206) 813-5645 (fax)
(800) 601-0070 (toll free)
Bangelson (e-mail on AOL)

or

He can sometimes be found in the shadow of Mount Rainier overlooking the vastness of cyberspace:

World Wide Web   http:\www.mindbodytalk.com

Go and visit;

your messages will be given prompt and full attention.

To Order Your Copy of The Living Dreamer

Title	Price	Qty.	Amount
The Living Dreamer	$17.95		
Shipping & Handling	$2.95/Book		
8.2% Sales Tax in Washington State			
Total Amount Enclosed			

Payment by: ❏ Check (Please make checks payable to Do It Publications.)
❏ Bank Card: ❏ Visa ❏ MasterCard
Bank Card # _____
Exp. Date _____
Name on Card _____
Signature _____

Please send to:
Name _____
Address _____
City _____ State _____ Zip _____
Phone _____ Fax _____

Return Order Form to:
Do It Publications, Inc. International;
PO Box 236; Kent, WA 98035
Phone 206-859-1714; Fax 206-813-5645

Orders will not be processed without payment.
Allow 2-4 weeks for delivery.
Quantity discounts available.